"As a working mom and self-proclaim
has given me the time and space to refl
path. I realized that the expectations I had held for myself were and not aligned with my long-term goals. With her encouragement, I could set boundaries with my time and refocus on the people and goals that were truly important to me. Kathy's keen and kind observations empowered me to let go of behaviors that no longer served me."

– Consulting Director,
Professional Services Company, and Working Mom

"Working with Kathy as my leadership development coach helped me take a realistic view of all that I am and all that I do. For the first time in a long time, I was able to see myself not just through the lens of my obligations, but as an individual, with my own needs and wants, my own dreams and goals. Getting back to basics – defining and affirming my personal values, remembering my aspirations from way back when, and finding inner strength and power – led me to a clear vision of the life I want. Kathy has been a true partner on my journey to self-rediscovery and to the life I want and deserve."

– Vice President,
Financial Services Company, and Working Mom

"As I reflect on our time together, I realized that prior to our engagement, I was going through motions, prioritizing others' needs before mine and not recognizing that to be fulfilled as a person, I needed more from myself, and to do that I needed to focus on myself and what I wanted out of my career and, frankly, out of life. My professional journey was so rooted in what I needed to do for others that it felt unnatural to shift focus to what I needed to do for myself.... Now, I am focusing on the things that matter most to me, my family, and my personal life, without compromising. I am allowing others to step up and step into situations that previously I thought only I could handle at work and making room for their growth both personally and professionally. The most important learning from our sessions was focused on me, the person, not what I do but what I want to do."

– Vice President,
Global Technology Company, and Working Mom

Moms
Eat First

5 PRINCIPLES TO PRIORITIZE YOURSELF AND CREATE THE CHANGE YOU CRAVE

KATHY SULLIVAN

BOARD CERTIFIED COACH AND PROSCI® CERTIFIED
CHANGE MANAGEMENT PRACTITIONER

PERFORMANCE
PUBLISHING

For moms who are ready to prioritize themselves.

Contents

PRINCIPLE #1:
Reflection is key to self-preservation.

PRINCIPLE #2:
Rediscovering possibilities is essential to feeding your soul

PRINCIPLE #3:
It's never too late to reset priorities based
on what is important to you.

PRINCIPLE #4:
Amid adversity, you can reclaim power through choice.

PRINCIPLE #5:
Peace prevails when you release what you can't control.

Preface

I've lost count of the number of times I've eaten my dinner standing up in the kitchen while splitting my focus among ten different things. Here's a prime example of what dinner looks like in our home:

I'm home after an impossibly long day at work. Instead of collapsing, I go all-out for my seventeen-year-old daughter and eight-year-old son—I grill chicken, roast broccoli, and boil white sticky rice—one of Brooke's favorites (drenched in soy sauce). In walks my son, Parker, who starts complaining about what I'm making; he doesn't eat chicken (at least on *that* day he doesn't). Parker prefers to graze throughout the day. So, instead of having an actual meal, he stomps out of the kitchen into the TV room and screams for me to cut an apple into slices and sprinkle cinnamon on top. Now, I know what you must be thinking, "An apple isn't dinner." And while I know that is the case, you must understand my son. For Parker, an innocent tiny apple easily transforms into an angry barrel of apples. So, I let it go—knowing that in about twenty minutes, he'll be asking—I mean screaming—for me to get him something more.

Throughout all of this, our dog, Nova, stands at the sliding glass door, wanting to go outside. Her way of informing us that she needs to go out is by tapping her nails on the glass. As you can imagine, it's like nails on a chalkboard. "What did you eat for dinner that night?" you ask. Three stalks of leftover broccoli, a spoonful of rice, and a glass of wine. Okay, maybe two glasses. I didn't even put the food on a plate. I grabbed the pot the broccoli was cooked in and took the last bite of rice left from Brooke's plate.

One thing hasn't changed over the years in my house...I'm the last one to eat. Always.

What I finally realized is that I often ate while standing at the counter. Rarely did I truly savor my food, or the moment, to stay present. Looking back, however, I see I was only trying to survive—nothing more.

Why on earth would I want to go through all the hassle of preparing a second meal just for me? I simply did not have the time, and honestly, I didn't have the energy. I was sleep-deprived. The mere thought of standing in the kitchen to organize a nice meal sounded daunting on many days. Standing and eating allowed me to quickly complete dinner and move on to the next thing that was on my to-do list. I felt like a robot...a highly efficient robot, but still, a robot. A robot that had lost all sense of feeling and was simply functioning on autopilot throughout each day.

Maybe I was tired from sitting all day at work, wracking my brain, which never turns off. It was constantly running through the list of things left undone or problems left unsolved. Things like going to the store, cleaning the house, filling out the online documents for both kids for school, scheduling doctor's appointments, finding a dog sitter so I could go visit my dad in New York, and finishing projects for my clients...the list goes on.

Or maybe I knew that the minute I sat down, there would be something else I would remember I needed to be doing. Or, more likely, I would get the millionth request from one of my kids to help them or get something for them. Or maybe I avoided the opportunity to sit and enjoy a meal because I knew if I did, I just might not be able to get back up from being so exhausted. I could never just simply *be*. Does this sound familiar to you?

I suspect you know Ralphie's mom in the movie *A Christmas Story*. Remember the part where she has just finished making dinner and sits down to eat? Before her fork reaches her mouth, her husband asks for a second serving of cabbage. She gets up and dishes out more cabbage. As soon as she sits back down, Ralphie asks for something, too. Then comes the voiceover, the adult Ralphie speaking. "My mother hadn't had a hot meal for herself in fifteen years," he says. I have watched that movie at least thirty times over the years. Only recently did I realize the significance of that scene and how much I can relate to it.

Working a full-time job, preparing meals at home, driving kids to and from activities, attending school meetings, making and attending appointments, and taking care of the house, and the dog— it is no wonder I have lost myself. It feels like I am constantly serving others and running on empty. By the time I realize I haven't done much for myself, I have nothing left to give. At times, I have had to sacrifice my basic needs: sleep, exercise, and eating right. How did I get to this place?

Like all people, I was a product of my environment. Your mom, or whoever you considered to be your parental figure, likely had a strong influence on how you parent your own children. I look back at my youth and my mom, Mary, in such a different light today. Had I known what was ahead in Mom's life and my own, I would have paid more attention to the little things she did and expressed more appreciation at the time.

My parents divorced when I was very young. So, my mom was a single parent raising my older sister, Christine, and me. I grew up in upstate NY and while my dad, Joe, was present in our lives, he spent time working out west for many years to provide for us. He therefore wasn't around much to help out with the day-to-day parenting responsibilities. This meant my mom had full responsibility for my sister and me.

My mom worked full-time for over thirty years at General Electric. I can vividly remember her coming home from work and being exhausted on most days. At times, I would ask her to do things or take me places after work, and I can recall the look on her face. The drain of work and raising two girls on her own was easy to see: the dark circles under her eyes from the lack of sleep, her brown hair that was starting to go gray at the roots, and her brown eyes that started to tear up from the guilt of not being able to satisfy our every wish, which I now understand so clearly. She sacrificed so much for my sister and me. I just didn't understand how much back then.

My mom passed away from lung cancer in 2014. I realize now all the things I learned from her—lessons to apply as well as a deeper understanding of the choices I've made to become the person I want to be. I hope that with this book, I can effectively tell my mom's story, too, and thus the story of a generation of mothers who, by and large, did more for others than themselves.

With both of my children, I have maintained a career and have always loved my work. I spent over twenty-five years working in human resources leadership roles, consulting with leaders and collaborating on implementing large-scale changes in various industries. In every change initiative, as I worked to help hundreds and sometimes thousands of employees understand the vision for change and why it was necessary, what became evident was the need for change at the individual level. That required each person to know their own values and beliefs and understand how they aligned with those of the organization.

I spend a lot of time these days helping people understand how they fit within the change and gain clarity on their own role in making it happen. Now, as an Organizational Development Consultant and Executive Coach, I work with leaders, teams, and individuals to facilitate change.

Change is most often related to systems, processes, and people; that is, driving behavioral change in people. After all, an organization doesn't change unless the people inside it decide to. Our homes are no different. We can't expect our family members to change simply because we tell them to. And you can't change unless you want it, are ready for it, and are willing to do the work required.

My story may have been a bit untraditional compared to the fairytales I grew up with, but everything has worked together in perfect precision. I started my career in my twenties, had baby number one in my early thirties, and *then* got married. Got divorced. Focused on my career. Had baby number two (unmarried) and focused more on my career. Then, I quit a job that I loved, took some time off to figure myself out more, and started my own business. I will share my story, and those of others, in more detail throughout this book.

What I have learned from close friends, business acquaintances, clients, research, chats with neighbors, and through my own experiences, is that moms take on too much. I hear it nearly every day, not always in the form of complaints, but simply in daily downloads of Mom's Life. The reasons vary: maybe there's a personality style that accommodates the needs of others and wants to be liked by everyone. Maybe there's a need to control everything, preferring to do it yourself, so it's done "the right way". Or maybe, just maybe, it is the acceptance of roles society has placed on moms of having to be everything to everyone and now it has become standard. Possibly, it is all of those things for some of you. The result is that those around you are accustomed to the ways you strive; anytime you deviate outside the lines, people get upset, so you return to old habits.

The COVID-19 pandemic exacerbated the challenges so many women were already facing. Childcare responsibilities for many families, particularly moms, were a big part of that. Research showed that moms were more likely to carry the additional "load" of homeschooling children as well as other household responsibilities. For many moms, this was all while maintaining a full-time job. And, for some, they simply couldn't maintain it due to childcare issues further perpetuating the systems in place, and as a result, left the workplace.

Your role as a mom certainly requires you to take care of others and to make sacrifices. But when you pile that responsibility on top of the other jobs: paid work, partnering, caring for aging parents, and the load that more often falls on moms, it can begin to feel like there's nothing left of yourself for *you.*

If this resonates with you, I encourage you to read on. You don't have to stay stuck on the proverbial hamster wheel every day. There is a way through the chaos, and this book will provide you with a framework to begin the process. The rest, my dear friends, is up to you!

Are you ready to elevate yourself?

Acknowledgements

I wish my mom was still alive so that I could tell her the positive impact she had on my life. I would prepare a couple of her favorite things—cinnamon coffee cake and a cup of hazelnut coffee. I would let her eat first.

I owe a lifetime of gratitude to my family for their support, teachings, and the happy memories we have had over the years.

- My mom, Mary, taught me to be kind and compassionate and to persevere, no matter what obstacles I faced. She instilled a foundation of faith that has provided the strength I've needed to get through life's challenges; I rely on that faith daily. I'm grateful for the example she set that has helped me become who I am.

- My dad, Joe, instilled great strength, determination, and discipline in me. He taught me life skills that allowed me to build confidence and gain agency over my life. He taught me to be tough and stand on my own. He always provided for his family and I hope he knows how grateful I am for all he has done.

- My "sissy", Christine, provides me with support, love, laughter, and home-cooked meals. She is the best auntie my kids could ever ask for. I would not be where I am today without having her by my side. She may never truly understand how much I've looked up to her, and how much her support has helped me through life's challenges.

- My favorite daughter, Brooke, has taught me to be more accountable and to live life abundantly, and authentically. I am in awe of her kindness, sense of humor, and intelligence. I am so proud of the woman she is becoming and know she will have an amazing impact on this world.

- My favorite son, Parker, has taught me more about patience and forgiveness and has offered me a front-row seat in the school of life. He fiercely challenges me to be a better mom every day. I know he will be a strong force in this world and hope he does so in his intelligent, unique, funny, and charismatic way.

- Special thanks to some wonderful women who supported me on my writing journey:

  o Michelle Prince, who inspired me to take a leap of faith and write this book.
  o Lisa Bess Kramer, who guided my early ideas and provided support.
  o Kimberly Hawkins, who helped me generate ideas and provided accountability.
  o Christa Parravani, who provided the structure I needed and brought my voice to life. You were a true gift and helped me get this book over the finish line.

Introduction

Have you come to a crossroads where a decision needs to be made to minimize the chaos and start elevating yourself as a priority? It's a simple idea that can feel impossible to implement. There are some key things I have learned over the years—as a mom, coach, friend, and family member, and just being human. Some of those lessons I have summarized for you below, in no particular order; some are further articulated in the chapters that follow.

Life Lessons

1. **Know who you are—flaws and all**. Understand your values and what is truly important. Love yourself—then decide what parts you want to protect, and which must be pruned.
2. **We act out of fear or love**. Choose love and stay in alignment with your values, while respecting the values of others—especially when they conflict with your own.
3. **Forgive others**. People generally don't do things to intentionally hurt; rather they act on what is hurting them—just like you. Forgive the transgressions of others and move on.

4. **Set healthy boundaries**. Make decisions that align with who you want to be and teach others where your guardrails are. Then provide feedback when people cross them.

5. **Know what grounds you**. You can expect a shit-storm to hit now and then. Know what keeps your feet planted on the ground, or at least what helps bring them back down.

6. **Simplify decision-making**. Explore ways to make decisions easier. Create repeatable processes and put systems and structures in place to save brain space. You will need it for more important things.

7. **Slow down to speed up.** Not everything needs to be done today. Sometimes you need to slow down to gain perspective and take inventory. You might realize things aren't that important or urgent.

8. **Watch your tongue**. Words matter. Ask yourself if what you are about to say will move you closer to who you want to be and the relationship you want to build with others—or drive you further away.

9. **Have faith in what *could* be**. You likely thought you would never get through past difficulties—but you are still here. New challenges will arise. Trust in your abilities and believe in possibilities.

10. **Take care of your mind, body, and spirit.** As long as you are able, it is your responsibility to take care of yourself—all parts. No one will put you first as well as you can.

11. **Meet people where they are**. Stop expecting people to do things *your* way and for *your* reasons. Understand what is important to them and what they need, and lean in.

12. **Hold yourself accountable**. You know what you need to do. Commit to and execute what you expect from yourself—it's much better than dealing with the consequences.

13. **Forgive yourself**. Give yourself grace when you make mistakes; it facilitates internal peace. Identify the lesson, find the humor in the situation, and let it go.

14. **Apologize when you hurt people**. Take responsibility when you hurt others and ask for forgiveness. This informs them you are taking accountability and is a step to restore trust and the relationship. Then act accordingly. The rest is up to them.

15. **Love others unconditionally**. As human beings everyone needs love and each person deserves it, regardless of where they come from or what they do. Including you. Love anyway. Then, read Life Lesson #3 again.

16. **Unplug regularly**. Step back now and then to reflect and gain perspective. Every minute of every day was not meant to be spent on getting something done. Enjoy the silence, just be, and allow for creativity. Your brain, body, and soul will thank you.

17. **Focus on what is important**. Stop making everything so urgent. Define your priorities and align your days accordingly. The other stuff is just fluff.

18. **Understand your feelings when communicating**. It's not other people who cause you to feel the way you do; it's the story you are telling yourself. Challenge your assumptions to ensure you are dealing with facts, then be clear about what you need and ask for it.

19. **Create a good support system**. Surround yourself with people you trust, who will give constructive feedback and encourage you to achieve the desires of your heart.

20. **Cultivate relationships.** Invest time in building relationships and be open to meeting people who are different from you. You can learn a lot through their experiences—and in

the process become more accepting of the things that make us all unique.

Throughout this book, you will learn strategies you can apply to your work and home life that will undoubtedly create discomfort. If you want change in your life, start getting comfortable with being uncomfortable. The framework I'm providing you with will require experimenting, and updated iterations applied repeatedly. I suggest you work through these principles in order from one through five and repeat, as needed. Some chapters may not apply to everyone, so feel free to skip those as you see fit.

It is also important for me to note that you are embarking on a potentially wild ride, as those around you may not be as committed to it as you. So, give them space and time to adjust to what they are hearing and seeing, as you start shifting your environment and inner self. They may not have the same motivation and may not hear the whispers that you are feeling and hearing. Stay true to yourself and be open to what your new pathway is sharing, while also tuning into the voice within you.

I acknowledge that I am a privileged white woman—*and* I have had many challenging life experiences, particularly as a single mom. I wrote this book for moms based on my own lived experiences, the experiences of those I have worked with, and what so much research shows regarding challenges women—particularly moms—encounter. I believe it is important to be vulnerable and share part of my story, and others', to shed light on those lived experiences. At the same time, know that I'm learning to own my narrative and that requires me to be thoughtful and selective about what parts of me I want to share to help others—and which parts I want to keep private. I hope you understand that is where I am on my journey.

Last, I will refer to "women" or "moms" in this book when it relates to specific research or examples. However, it would be remiss of me not to point out that the topics I will discuss, and the principles I will share, apply to other people regardless of how you identify. Because of that, I will also refer to "people" or "person(s)", to be inclusive of others who may relate and have similar lived experiences. Whether that includes dads, grandparents, someone who identifies as non-binary, or anyone else—this is also for you.

Seasons of Life

We all go through seasons in our lives, especially women. You might be leaning all the way in, leaning halfway in, leaning all the way out, or leaning out with your head tipped back with arms and legs sprawled in front of you because you are so exhausted...again. It is important that we not only appreciate our seasons in life but take advantage of them. Whether you are pregnant now or looking to adopt, a new mother with an infant or toddler, or a parent to older kids and preparing to become an empty nester, each season is different, has challenges, and requires something unique from you as a mom. Regardless of what season you are in, take time to understand who you are and what you want for yourself. Recognize that will also change as you enter new seasons. No one else can—or will—do it for you.

So many women I know and have coached have been in survival mode for so long that they have forgotten how to explore the possibilities that exist in their future. This book will not give you the answers—those are for you to find. Rather, it will provide a framework and offer questions to help you learn more about yourself, define what you want, and better prepare you for overcoming obstacles that get in the way of achieving what you want.

This is not about you finding your purpose as a mom, a partner, or a career professional. It is about rediscovering what makes you feel alive and helping you explore the possibilities that exist to achieve your next level of potential based on what is important to you. This will require you to put yourself first, which will undoubtedly make some of you extremely uncomfortable. Not to mention, it will demand hard work. Moreover, it will rely on your willingness to dig deep into places you may have kept hidden.

There are five key principles I will share with you, which are briefly described below, that will help you navigate the change you crave. These principles provide a framework to facilitate the change you want to see for yourself. They revolve around acting on the Five R's, which requires you to: reflect, rediscover, reset, reclaim, and release. Each principle will be expanded on in the sections that follow, through stories, defining the real issue women face, and providing you with a starting point, should you choose to do the work. The five principles are:

PRINCIPLE #1:
Reflection *is key to self-preservation.*

PRINCIPLE #2:
Rediscovering *possibilities is essential to feeding your soul.*

PRINCIPLE #3:
It's never too late to **reset** *priorities based on what is important to you.*

PRINCIPLE #4:
Amid adversity, you can **reclaim** *power through choice.*

PRINCIPLE #5:
Peace prevails when you **release** *what you can't control.*

You may wonder why these principles begin with the prefix "re", which means "again" or "repeat". The purpose of this is that our personal and professional growth is a journey that is often not linear. Rather, our lives experience ups and downs and will require multiple iterations of these five principles. Likely you have already discovered possibilities in your life and set goals to achieve your dreams. But your life is constantly evolving and so much can shift, so you must be prepared to adapt as well.

When obstacles come your way, you need to be prepared to stand your ground, remind yourself what you are working toward, and reclaim what is yours for the taking. At times, you may have to accept that you are where you are for a reason—what I sometimes refer to as the "shit-show". If you don't sit in it long enough to figure out how you are really feeling, how can you ever identify and deal with the *real* issue?

There may be something you need to learn or experience that will help you grow and prepare for the future. You will need to capture the lesson the experience is trying to give—a gift. The gift may be one of increased patience, resilience, or clarity.

I expect these principles will provide you with better insight into who you are and what you want and inspire action toward your personal vision.

In the end, we all have to put in the hard work and take deliberate and decisive action—while recognizing that which we need to let go. That might include finding a new career, staying home to raise your children, going back to work, getting a degree, dating someone new, or getting out of a toxic relationship.

The work you need to do might be difficult for some of you because it requires you to actually consider how you are *really* feeling deep down. It will require you to consider what you believe in—not what others say you should believe in. It will require you to do things differently and may require you to communicate differently, which may cause discomfort in people close to you.

By acting, new opportunities and information will be revealed as to the next steps, but you may not see them from where you stand today. This is why it is key to continue moving forward so that the right path will appear, so you can develop strength and confidence in the process.

I encourage you to revisit these five principles based on where you are in life and what you want or need. Life throws curveballs and requires us to shift at times. These principles will help you navigate those experiences and create a framework to operate within.

Science Behind the Madness

Moms are conditioned to put the needs of others before their own. This has likely contributed to the saying "moms know best" and developing the ability to nurture others. It is also a foundation for what can become an over-practiced strength that has the potential to become a development opportunity. When moms consistently put the needs of others above their own, especially at the expense of getting their own basic needs met, it can contribute to burnout, stress, and resentment. Not to mention, it can be associated with depression and other challenges that impact mental, physical, emotional, and overall well-being. Following the pandemic, moms face the largest rates of anxiety and depression, which can include increased rates of alcohol and substance addictions and suicide.[1]

One thing I was not so surprised to learn is that science plays a part in developing the desire to nurture others. What is to blame for that? Certain chemicals, including endorphins, dopamine, serotonin, and oxytocin are involved. Below is a brief description of each, and its impact on our bodies:

Endorphins: hormones made in your brain that act as messengers throughout the body. They are produced to help relieve physical pain, reduce stress, and improve mood. There are various things you can do to increase endorphin levels such as getting a massage, exercising, and even having sex. A "runner's high" is a good example of how this hormone impacts the body.

Dopamine: a neurotransmitter released by the brain. It is known as the "feel good" hormone and part of the reward system. When you do something enjoyable, it gives you a feeling of satisfaction—it can also motivate action. An example of how this affects the body is the enjoyment people get from checking things off a written to-do list. It makes you feel like you accomplished a thing or two. Or, in a mom's case, twenty things!

One downside is that dopamine can be highly addictive. You might experience this yourself when viewing how many likes you received from that post on Facebook, Instagram, or other social media platforms. Another example is the sense of reward you may get from helping others.

Serotonin[2]: a neurotransmitter that carries messages in our bodies. This can help balance endorphins and dopamine. It influences memory and happiness and supports the regulation of sleep and hunger.

Oxytocin[3]: a chemical that acts as a messenger and contributes to behaviors related to social interactions like trust, and as fate would have it, bonding with infants. It is this chemical that helps moms during childbirth as well as lactation. When you think about it, moms sacrifice themselves for their babies. The challenge is the more you do for others, the more you want to do for others. You can thank oxytocin for that, moms!

During pregnancy, a woman's brain experiences changes that contribute to increased social awareness. According to neuroscience research, neural networks that are focused on social cognition experience reorganization. As a result, women have a heightened sensitivity and response readiness that relate to cues in others, such as when a baby cries.[4]

In other words, pregnancy prepares a woman for parenting, allowing her to be empathetic and attentive to others.

I suspect this experience has also translated into the workplace as well. It may be why research also showed that during the pandemic women were more likely to provide emotional support to others—there was no "off" switch to the "mommy brain". I can't help but wonder how much of this natural order of things impacts a woman's focus on prioritizing herself.

I am *not* suggesting that moms stop taking care of others. That would negatively impact the healthy contributions many women make in the family structure, organizations, and communities around the world. It is, in my opinion, part of how moms add tremendous value to society and in the workplace.

What I *am* suggesting is that you take inventory of where you are and gain an understanding of what drives your behavior. When you better understand yourself and why you do what you do, you can begin to make choices that align with what you want to achieve in life.

I have broken this book into five main sections, and each includes three chapters. The first chapter will be a personal experience or client story that will illustrate the principle in practice. The second chapter will be coaching that works through the principle, so you can gain insight into how the tools are applied and relate to the story that was shared. The last chapter of each section will be a workbook for you to *do the work*.

Buckle up, everyone. You are about to experience some turbulence ahead.

Endnotes

[1] Kweilin Ellingrud and Kunal Modi, "Meeting the Challenge of Moms' 'Double Double Shift' at Home and Work," McKinsey & Company, May 5, 2022, https://www.mckinsey.com/featured-insights/sustainable-inclusive-growth/future-of-america/meeting-the-challenge-of-moms-double-double-shift-at-home-and-work.

[2] Related resources:

- Arjun Bakshi, "Biochemistry, Serotonin," StatPearls [Internet], July 31, 2021, https://www.ncbi.nlm.nih.gov/books/NBK560856/.
- Matteo Briguglio et al., "Dietary Neurotransmitters: A Narrative Review on Current Knowledge," Nutrients, May 10, 2018, https://www.ncbi.nlm.nih.gov/pmc/articles/PMC5986471/.
- Endocrine Society, "Brain Hormones," January 24, 2022, https://www.hormone.org/your-health-and-hormones/glands-and-hormones-a-to-z/hormones/serotonin.
- Mendel Friedman, "Analysis, Nutrition, and Health Benefits of Tryptophan," International Journal of Tryptophan Research 11 (September 26, 2018): https://doi.org/10.1177/1178646918802282.
- Mark Gudesblatt, "You Ask. We Answer," Neurology Now 13, no. 3 (June 2017): 42, https://doi.org/10.1097/01.nnn.0000520752.91170.81.
- Lauren A. Jones, Emily W. Sun, Alyce M. Martin, and Damien J. Keating, "The Ever-Changing Roles of Serotonin," The International Journal of Biochemistry & Cell Biology 125 (August 2020): 105776, https://doi.org/10.1016/j.biocel.2020.105776.
- James Sonne, "Dopamine," StatPearls [Internet], July 3, 2023, https://www.ncbi.nlm.nih.gov/books/NBK535451/.
- Simon N. Young, "How to Increase Serotonin in the Human Brain without Drugs," Journal of Psychiatry & Neuroscience:

JPN, November 2007, https://www.ncbi.nlm.nih.gov/pmc/articles/PMC2077351/.

(3) Related resources:

- Osilla, Eva V. "Oxytocin." StatPearls [Internet]., July 24, 2023. Eva V. Osilla, "Oxytocin," StatPearls [Internet], July 24, 2023, https://www.ncbi.nlm.nih.gov/books/NBK507848/.
- "Oxytocin," You and Your Hormones, March 2019, https://www.yourhormones.info/hormones/oxytocin/.
- Hiran Patel, "Physiology, Posterior Pituitary," StatPearls [Internet], April 24, 2023, https://www.ncbi.nlm.nih.gov/books/NBK526130/.

(4) Sarah McKay, Baby Brain: The Surprising Neuroscience of How Pregnancy and Motherhood Sculpt Our Brains and Change Our Minds (For the Better) (Auckland, New Zealand: Hachette Aotearoa New Zealand, 2023).

PRINCIPLE #1

Reflection is key to self-preservation.

CHAPTER 1

Oh, Boy!

"The unexamined life is not worth living."
– Socrates

First things first. It is essential to tell you about how I arrived at a crisis in my life that forced me to put myself first.

I was in my mid-forties, a single parent to a daughter, and living a good life in Southern California. I was established in my career, had a great group of friends, was in great shape, and was doing my best to effectively co-parent with my ex-husband to raise our daughter. One of the greatest griefs of my divorce was that I had always envisioned having a large family. But, by that point in my life, I had put that want aside; it just wasn't in the cards for me. And then, on my journey to finding new love and a life partner, I got pregnant. By surprise. As much as I adored my partner, it was clear after I'd told him the news, I would be parenting on my own.

My initial thought was: "I can't do this alone." Then I said to myself: "I don't want to do this alone." I worried about how I would financially support this new child and my daughter on my own. I worried about how I was going to work and afford childcare and all the other expenses, responsibilities, and work that were necessary to raise a child. I worried if I would ever be able to be *me* again.

But, after a lot of reflection, sleepless nights crying uncontrolla-bly, endless prayers, and attempts at negotiating with God, I realized how lucky I was. I allowed myself to feel it all: worry, anticipation, shame, joy, despair, excitement. It was right for me to have this baby. I'd be all on my own, yes, but I summoned the pragmatist in me and set out to puzzle through my life.

I had some very grounding conversations with my sister and reflected on what I've always wanted: to be a mom and have multiple children. It didn't turn out the way I had planned, but it was what I wanted! And I was going to make it work. So, I strategized. But of course, as is the way of life, nothing is simple. There were other com-plicated factors during my pregnancy, namely, as I was welcoming a second child, my mom was diagnosed with lung cancer and was in treatment. And because I lived in California, my sister was bearing the brunt of caring for our mother back east.

At that time in my life, I essentially implemented the process, tools, and strategies that I help clients with today as a coach. To get what you want, you have to prioritize what is important to you—then work through logistics.

I asked myself: What do I need not only to survive, but thrive?

When it came down to it, I wanted to be with my family. I wanted to get back to an environment that more closely aligned with what I valued and that would offer the best support.

So, the first thing to go would be California. I'd been so fortu-nate. There I was, living alone in one of the most desirable neighbor-hoods in the country, a few miles from the beach in Laguna Niguel. My ex-husband lived a couple of blocks away, in a house so near to mine that he could see us. And yet, it's not what I wanted. Despite the great friends I had, the beautiful weather, and the paradisiacal lifestyle, I knew it wouldn't satisfy the craving in me and what I wanted, what I *needed*.

The next thing to go would be my job. I had a great role working as an Organizational Development Manager, which meant that I was responsible for driving key changes that would help develop people, such as leadership development programs, as well as implementing systems and processes to drive desired changes. I had the opportunity to create a framework for leaders by developing leadership competencies that defined desired behaviors, then creating talent review processes, training programs, and implementing tools to support people in their development. It was about facilitating organizational change at the individual level.

I was lucky to be working alongside my long-time mentor, whom I had followed to a technology services company. She was an amazing boss, and I was fortunate to have wonderful opportunities for growth under her leadership. But one thing I knew for sure, the business required that position to function in the corporate office in Irvine, California.

Soon after, I would experience one of the most difficult negotiations of my life: my ex-husband and I agreeing on relocating back to the east coast.

The surprise pregnancy offered so many blessings in disguise. For one, I'd be closer to family and able to spend more time with my mom as well. So, I made the decision to move to Ohio, where my sister resided. My form of self-care was going to be surrounding myself with family. Staying in California was not a healthy option for me. I knew deep down in my soul I was doing the right thing, but I wasn't able to breathe a sigh of relief quite yet. There was still so much to plan for, take care of, and muster through.

Over the next few weeks, I listed my house, planned a trip to Ohio to look at homes, and prepared to talk to my boss about quitting my job. That would prove to be one of the most difficult conversations in preparing for this next phase in my life.

Reflecting on My Most Important Assignment

"Take a deep breath, Kathy…deep breath. Breathe in slowly for four seconds and breathe out slowly for four seconds." I say this under my breath almost every day. I know the feeling of mom burnout all too well—exhausting every last bit of energy and using up any access to internal and external resources available—*if* available. Yet, many things are left undone and, even worse, not yet started. Sadly, important things are sometimes left unsaid, like "I love you" to my kids. I have found it hard to allow myself the little pleasures in life, all because I am spent, my memory bank is drained, and I am resentful about all the things I still must do…by myself.

In my life, I have the primary responsibility of taking care of two children. My daughter, Brooke, who is the oldest, is in her first year of college. My son, Parker, is in fourth grade. Both are smart and funny and have their own very distinct personalities, which are extremely different. As a result, I have had to adjust my parenting approach as what works with one child doesn't work with the other one.

I have worried that I failed as a parent on more days than I would like to admit. I feared I failed, but we all know that we are harder on ourselves than others, so I am not the failure I built myself up to be in my mind. Yet, it is amazing the power our thinking can have over us.

Let me share a little more insight into my story.

When my daughter, Brooke, was a toddler and before I had Parker, I remember vividly how my days unfolded, much like the actor in the old Dunkin' Donuts commercials I used to see when I was growing up. The gentleman with the dark hair and mustache would presumably roll out of bed at 3:00 a.m. He got dressed with only one eye open, and slowly shuffled his way to work, saying in a drawn-out, monotone, tired voice, "Time to make the donuts."

Back then, I used to get up well before her to steal time for myself. Working through my laundry list of to-dos—paying bills, answering emails, working on projects that required my focus and intellect, you name it. At that time, I had a job I enjoyed, but required some travel, making it hard to feel like I was being the best mom I could be. Of course, a mom's guilt can go far and deep in multiple directions if it's not cornered and tamed.

Looking back on those days, I was always in a rush. Everything had to be done quickly, and I often felt I was always running out of time. I tended to race through life feeling a perpetual sense of urgency. I can hear my mom saying, "Patience is a virtue, Kathy," or, "Slow down." I felt judged by that voice. Having my second child would prove even more challenging, especially as a single parent and trying to do everything on my own. The negative stories I played in my mind were paralyzing me and robbing my children of their mother…the real mother I truly was, instead of the mother who didn't always show up as she wanted—or needed to.

The road to parenthood was a bit rocky for this single, full-time working mom. Now, I find myself impressed with how far I have come and the bravery I had—and still have—to stand firm for what I want. Sometimes, I have settled for less than I desired and deserved, and for what I now believe God has intended for my life. I have learned some critical lessons over the years that have allowed me to keep moving forward and gain strength.

My bravery continues to this day as I work hard to show up as I am meant to be, and want to be, for the benefit of myself, my kids, my friends and family, and my clients—no matter what. The uncomfortable part is that this involves taking care of myself as a priority. If I don't, who will?

The level of responsibility I carry (both physically and mentally) means I'm essentially "on" 24/7, 365 days a year. I say 365 days, but I am a master at pushing 730 days' worth of value into those 365 days. If you are a mom, I bet you can relate to some of this, regardless of whether you work outside the home, are married, or have an only child. Being a mom is one of the most challenging jobs anyone could have…and, in my opinion, is also the most rewarding.

Some terms have been used to describe this experience moms have of bearing the brunt of responsibility at home and work, which often manifests itself into a whole new level of work. These terms include the "mental load" and the "third shift". This became even more prevalent during the pandemic, when women were more than *three times* as likely as men to be responsible for most housework and caregiving in households with two heterosexual parents. Working mothers have to deal with paid work, household responsibilities, mental challenges, and dealing with other family circumstances. Many of these issues are further exacerbated for women of color and single mothers.[5]

Regardless of your living situation, think of the changes COVID-19 brought to our lives and how we operate on a day-to-day basis. Whether it was dealing with a partner working from home and taking up the space that used to provide some solace or the fact that you had to become a full-time teacher and homeschool your kids—all while you also did your paid job.

For some, it was a few of those things. For others, every responsibility fell on them, and them alone. I felt the blow as I tried to have private conversations with my clients, all while desperately wanting to scream "BE QUIET and STOP FIGHTING!" into the other room…while I'm on camera, no less. I admit, there may have been an instance or two where I did scream that, and maybe someone did hear me because I wasn't on mute!

I did not have a partner to watch the kids during my crucial client meetings…it was all on me, which continues to this day. I have made it through and know I will continue to persevere. And for those of you in similar situations, I genuinely believe you can, too, with the right resources and tools.

Moms learn to become great multi-taskers, demonstrate extraordinary compassion toward others, and develop a sixth sense to pick up on the needs of others. With the suitable capacity and resources, some moms can run circles around just about anyone. Being a mom is the most impressive thing I have ever accomplished…well-surpassing my most impressive professional accolades.

In a world that often looks to moms to be the primary caretakers, always helping everyone around them, it is no wonder moms have one of the highest burnout rates, experience bouts of depression, and may resort to substance abuse to cope. There are many resources out there to help moms that can make a difference in their lives. Yet many women are unaware of the resources, are too embarrassed to ask for help, or find it impossible to prioritize the time to take advantage of them. Others may still be in the honeymoon stage of motherhood and do not see the need for them quite yet. If that is you, consider yourself lucky! I hope that it continues for you.

I cannot read one more email at the end of some days…no matter how helpful. Yes, I could depend on others and, at times, do. The "mom guilt" that can come with "allowing" others to help us can also be excruciating. This book is for moms, but I know there are other people out there who may not identify as a "mom" and who are carrying similar responsibilities. Ultimately, I remind myself that I can't continue to operate at this pace if I don't let go of *something*. To do this, I must change my behavior and mindset. I must figure out who I am and what I want and identify how to get there. The five principles I share in this book help you with the "how".

The Road to Parenthood

At times, I think back to who I was before becoming a mom. I think about the freedom I felt and being able to discover new things without having to consider much or the needs of another person other than myself. The control that I had over my days and my environment. I think about the independence I had in how I spent my days. I have always been an adventurous and curious person, so packing for a last-minute trip for a long weekend was exciting. Or, simply going out shopping with friends for the afternoon and having dinner. These days, doing those things takes a lot more planning in advance, and the cost is a lot more for me. Even going out to have dinner with a friend can cost a month's worth of groceries for me after paying a babysitter these days.

I also think about how I was treated before having kids…compared to how I am treated now, as a mom. Especially a single mom. It is interesting how married couples rarely invite the single mom to dinners, happy hours, or parties. There must be something about always having an even number.

Then, I daydream about the past when my body looked different and how I worked so hard to keep in good shape, but it was still relatively easy to look good in years past…well, compared to now, anyway (thank you, mother nature, gravity, and hormones!). I think about what was important to me then, which now seems so incredibly irrelevant. I often reflect on the things I used to worry about in life…I was so naive in what comes to mind as I remember meltdowns over bad hair days, not fitting into my jeans, the guy not texting me back, or worrying about what someone else said about me behind my back.

I absolutely love being a mom. But not necessarily hearing the word "Mom!" shouted repeatedly from downstairs as I am upstairs trying to take a few minutes to myself. But yes, it is the most wonderful word to hear from another human being, and it is a huge responsibility. Being a mom pales in comparison to any other "job". I recognize the tremendous blessings my children are to me. I am forever grateful for the experience of being a mom. But I can tell you that I did not always feel like I excelled at the role, and some days I didn't want the responsibilities it brought. Sometimes I felt it would ruin me. Some days, it nearly did.

These days, everything looks a lot different to me now that I am a mom. No matter how hard I try, the respect I believe I gave my parents growing up does not look the same in my household, at least *some* days, that is.

At times I experience entitlement, lack of appreciation, and unkind words. Admittedly, I can contribute to this as well. In full candor, if you are a new mom embarking on this journey, the days of having any semblance of control are pretty much gone. And, if you are like me, you quickly develop wrinkles in your face from all the frowning and screaming you do at your kids. The physical, emotional, and mental load is real. It has taken a long time for me to relax because even when the kids are somewhere else—they are on my mind.

You may feel the same and find yourself asking, "Are they okay?" or, "Did they eat breakfast this morning?" or, "Did they take their coat to school?" because it is freezing outside. I don't know about you, but the moment I became a mom was when everything changed for me, especially the first time I could feel them moving inside my belly. From that moment on, I felt my life was no longer my own. I would forever be serving the needs of my children…first.

I find that as I grow older and further into parenthood, every year I start to respect the responsibility of being a parent more and more. I understand how fleeting it can be, which keeps me focused on being present and taking in all that I can, even in times of complete chaos. Keeping it all in perspective in each season of parenthood is critical to our survival and ability to be effective. Now, I remind myself of what I truly have control over and work to prepare them better as they grow into who they are meant to be.

Beliefs Passed On

I learned a lot from my mom, Mary. She was one of a kind. She was thoughtful, giving, and pragmatic. She was a woman with strong faith yet she had a great sense of humor. When my sister, Christine, and I would get in trouble, my mom would snap her fingers and then extend her arm, pointing to our bedrooms and would say, "Go to your room!" At times, we would mimic those movements and repeat her words, and she would start laughing with us. It didn't work every time, but it was a great strategy to get out of any disciplinary action. I catch myself now and then saying the same thing to my kids that my mom said to my sister and me, like, "My nerves are shot!" It was my mom's kinder approach to saying, "Shut up!"

Aside from the wonderful—and not so wonderful—qualities my mom had, I also realized that she served everyone around her. In hindsight, I now see where I developed some of my own parenting tendencies.

My parents divorced when I was very young, so growing up all I really knew was the life of a single-mom household. My sister Christine is a few years older than me, and while my father, Joe, supported and contributed to raising us, we spent most of our time living with my mom—at least until our high school years.

When my mom did try to do things for herself—like date men—I didn't necessarily support it. I don't recall my mom dating that much, but I vividly recall her spending time with a man named Hank. He was very tall and charming and seemed to treat my mom very well. I can remember her smiling more and relaxing a bit more when he was around. She was taking time to do things she enjoyed more, which didn't always include my sister and me. It was a transition I wasn't necessarily ready for, but one that my mom I'm sure so desperately needed and wanted. Dating allowed her to gain independence from her parenting responsibilities, it built her confidence, and in many ways probably gave her a sense of freedom she hadn't felt in a long time. Ironically, those are the very same feelings I have had myself, since I started dating again after my divorce.

For whatever reason, my mom's relationship with Hank didn't last.

My mom went on to meet her second husband, Ray, years later at church. They got married when I was in my early teens and remained married until my mom passed away. Even through their relationship, I can remember feeling like I was no longer important to my mom. It was as if I was watching her life move on without me. I suspect I felt that way because my mom and Ray got married rather quickly after meeting, and the only time I felt included in any conversation was when they both sat down at dinner with my sister and me to inform us of their engagement. She obviously knew he was the one for her because they remained married for well over thirty years. It was an unexpected change though, so for me, I wasn't fully bought in. As a result, it took a long time to build and rebuild those relationships and trust, as well as learn from the experience.

Had I known then what I know now, I would have realized my mom was simply trying to prioritize herself, her dreams, and desires, and still be the best mom she could be, given her circumstances. But having my own life experiences and reflecting on what my mom did, and what she taught me, has opened my eyes. Now I know better, so I can do better.

Despite how great I believe my mom was, I have also realized that I am my own person. I may carry on some of her tendencies and traditions and do a few things just like she did, but there are also things that I need to learn on my own. I had to figure out what was important to me and recognize what *I* valued. This meant I had to break free from what my mom and dad thought was best for me. I had to evaluate if what I believed in was truly what I believed in, or if I was simply carrying on their values and beliefs. For me, some of their beliefs were no longer serving me and what I wanted for myself.

I had to reflect on my priorities, my core values, and what I see as important given my circumstances, as a mom and as an individual.

My parents went through a lot of hardships. Though we weren't necessarily poor by most standards, we certainly weren't rich either. I would say we were probably a lower middle-class family, and one particular life-changing event was, I believe, a catalyst that changed the trajectory of all of our lives.

When my sister was about two, and my mom was pregnant with me, there was a horrible flood in Corning, NY, where the family was living at the time. From what I remember my parents telling me, the flood water was so high, they had to be taken out of the second-floor apartment through the windows and placed in a boat. I know it was that experience, and likely other issues within their marriage, that led my mom to surrender her life and become a born-again Christian.

Growing up, my mom didn't do anything without asking Jesus first. On days when she found a parking spot near the entrance of a busy shopping plaza, she thanked Him for finding it. My sister and I had many laughs over the years about that! But in hindsight, I realize her relationship with Jesus was what got her through each day.

When I was younger, I didn't understand why my mom had what seemed to be an over-reliance on her beliefs. Quite honestly, it was often embarrassing for me. Anytime I had a friend over, my mom would try to convert them to becoming "born-again". She would ask to pray over people, and even though it was evident others were uncomfortable with it, she would pray for them anyway.

This was difficult as a child and growing up into a young adult, as I was still figuring out myself and trying to fit in socially. I didn't fully buy into the whole idea of *her* religious beliefs. Honestly, I didn't really understand it at the time. As I have gotten older and had various life experiences, I have developed a lot more empathy for what my mom went through on her own and raising two girls. I wish that she was still here to talk about my struggles, to gain her perspective, even just to hear her say, "This, too, shall pass, Kathy." While I have some of the same beliefs my mom did, I no longer compare myself to her, as I am on my own path. In some ways, I looked at my mom like she did nothing wrong, when in fact, she had her faults just like me.

While I know my mom never meant to be disrespectful toward others, she could be judgmental at times. It was almost like she felt her religion gave her permission to force her beliefs on others. It took a long time, lots of reflection, and plenty of therapy to figure out what I believe. I do believe in God, and I respect the beliefs of others. I don't force my beliefs on others, but I will share what I believe He has done in my life. This realization would only come to me with time, reflection, and digging deep to think about who I am and what I believe.

In the past, I was still living my life through the lens of what both my mom and my dad wanted for me, instead of what I really wanted and believed for myself. With good intention, many parents instill their own beliefs in their kids—be it their cultural traditions, family values, religious values, etc. And unless you take time to sit down as an adult and really explore what you believe in and what values you want to live by, you very well may be living for, and through, someone else.

Are you minimizing your values, beliefs, and dreams, to keep the peace, or to make others feel less insecure about themselves? Do you know what you value?

When you take time to reflect on what your values are and what you believe in, it is much easier to align your choices. What you learn after reflecting on these things will create a foundation for everything you do going forward.

Endnotes

(5)   Jess Huang et al., "For Mothers in the Workplace, a Year (and Counting) Like No Other," McKinsey & Company, May 5, 2021, https://www.mckinsey.com/featured-insights/diversity-and-inclusion/for-mothers-in-the-workplace-a-year-and-counting-like-no-other.

CHAPTER 2

Numb

*"I've learned that you shouldn't go through life
with a catcher's mitt on both hands; you need
to be able to throw something back."*
– Maya Angelou, Author

Women are finding themselves in unplanned crisis mode and being defeated by the chiseling away of their self-agency. Many are operating on the proverbial hamster wheel every day, just trying to stay protected from all the balls thrown at them. The consequence? In short, not living the life they want for themselves. The various responsibilities coupled with the lack of prioritizing yourself can increase the risk of stress, depression, and substance abuse. Moms are already at relatively high risk of developing postpartum depression. Additionally, many parents are faced with navigating mental health issues in their children, who have also experienced significant struggles over the past few years and need help.

Women also face much more pressure compared to their male counterparts, particularly as it relates to being an involved parent. At the same time, there are unrealistic expectations of being and staying physically attractive. Add to that the unrealistic expectations when compared to other women who don't have the same demands.

Layering more, the expectation of intimacy with their partner at the end of a very long and stressful day—all without any effort by their partner to help relieve the "mental load"—and sometimes getting little in return. Yes, it is great to eat right, exercise, and stay generally healthy, but that is not enough—according to the pressures of social media, ad campaigns, and the perceived competition…*other women*.

The pressures are real and create unnecessary anxiety, so it is essential to recognize the emotions as they start to be felt. According to the Pew Research Center (2019):

- 77% of women surveyed said they felt pressure to be an involved parent compared to 49% of men.
- 71% of women reported feeling pressure to be physically attractive compared to 27% of men.

Although this research was done a few years ago, with the uptick in social media content, stories, and images, I suspect it hasn't changed all that much. When you couple these statistics with the images that are out there on social media and blogs about what a "good mom" is, what you *should* look like, or what other women are doing, it can be hard to feel successful…whether that is about looks, career, or the activity levels you maintain in the lives of your child(ren).

Additionally, many parents today are taking care of children who are neurodivergent and have unique differences and needs, such as with Attention Deficit Hyperactivity Disorder (ADHD) and Autism. Since COVID-19, many parents are also managing children suffering from anxiety and depression. If the women in those families are the primary caretakers, then they are likely handling those challenges at a disproportionate rate to their partners. For many women, they are doing their best, but without adequate resources to effectively handle the unique challenges that come along with parenting a child with special needs.

Furthermore, on average, women spend more hours on house-hold responsibilities than men. COVID-19 has widened this gap even further. In opposite-sex marriages, men spend considerably more time at work and on leisure activities than women. The way these couples divide their time remains unbalanced, according to recent research conducted by Pew Research Center (2023). Women carry a heavier load when it comes to chores in the home and care-giving responsibilities. For women of color, the gaps are even wider.[6]

Women are struggling and, to some extent, being left behind. Moms are facing declines in their careers, and their mental health is suffering. For many women, spending extra time on household responsibilities was "normal", so with the gap getting wider due to the pandemic, better support systems need to be put into place. I don't think we will ever see the same normalcy as we did before, but we can begin to shift the paradigm by resetting expectations of our-selves, and of others.

Figure 1. Super Mom Syndrome—a graphic representation of the responsibilities many moms face in their home and work life.

SUPER MOM SYNDROME

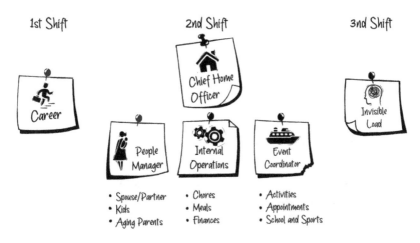

When you fail to take time to step back, consider what is on your plate, and identify how you are feeling, you run the risk of becoming numb to everything and everyone around you.

As I reflect on the various conversations with clients, friends, and family members who are moms, another common theme emerges of putting others first—consistently. This may take the form of doing everything at home rather than dividing responsibilities and partnering on all the tasks required to take care of kids and the home. During a presentation I have conducted for various organizations, "Making Work Work for Working Moms (pun intended)", I created the illustration above to demonstrate the "responsibilities" many moms face across work and home life.

Women may also feel the need to accommodate everyone else at work—taking on projects that are asked of them and volunteering for special projects that provide meaning but may result in no recognition or compensation. Or it can reflect in all the volunteering women may do, getting involved in too many things because they "want to help others".

There is nothing wrong with wanting to help others and doing so. But at what price? Consistently putting the needs of others first or accommodating people over time can contribute to increased stress and feelings of frustration or even resentment, not to mention a lack of fulfillment due to meeting everyone else's needs but your own.

So, what causes women to feel the need to put others first? Based on my research, experience, and discussions with moms, here are a few reasons that may resonate with you:

- **Reality of life:** Let's face it, we all have situations in our lives that require us to make sacrifices. Having children is no exception. Obviously, there are times (and sometimes seasons) when we need to put others first, and it's not always about the kids. Many people also have spouses, aging par-

20

ents, work outside the home, health conditions, and many other responsibilities. They find themselves unable to get out from under all the responsibility life brings, not to mention this is what society expects of women particularly…still. Hence, the next potential reason women put others first.

- **Gender roles:** The popular view of a mom's role in society is antiquated. While societal expectations might have shifted some from the idea that women belong in the kitchen barefoot and pregnant, we still have a way to go. Parents need to define the roles each partner will have based on what they feel is right for their family. If you are a stay-at-home mom and take on most responsibilities within the home while your partner works, great! If you are a single mom and hire someone part-time to help out with household chores and with the kids—or doing it all on your own, great! If you are a full-time working mom and your partner is the primary caretaker, great! The point here is obviously that there is no one right way to parent your children. Getting to a place of shared responsibility requires having some tough conversations and challenging not only societal norms, but what your partner, family members, neighbors, and even friends might feel is best. Establishing a system at home that is more fluid allows you to adapt to the season of life in which you find yourself and can be more sustainable.

- **Belief systems:** Our belief systems drive a lot of our behavior. They may come from convictions passed down by parents (with which you may or may not still agree), or from other societal expectations and influences. Or they may be a result of the dynamics of your relationship with your partner and what you have become accustomed to. When other people's beliefs differ from what you believe the role of a mom is, that creates friction in the relationship. There is a dynamic at play around what the mother's role is expected to be, and each couple has its own experiences and expectations. If you and your partner aren't aligned on your beliefs, that may be contributing to where you are at this moment.

- **"Good mom" syndrome**: If you look at how women are socialized about what a "good mom" looks like, many will say it's someone who spends a lot of quality time with kids, doing crafts, helping with homework, and maintaining strong emotional connections—all while doting on your partner and maintaining the perfect household (not to mention a perfect body that defies the typical aging process). You may worry that if you don't do "x, y, or z", you won't be seen as a "good mom" by others. This is about being everything to everyone all the time.

  There are so many factors that contribute to making a home a peaceful and high-functioning place—being organized, clarity about who does what (including the kids, if possible!), having fun, good communication, positive reinforcements, consequences, and a synergy that brings everything and everyone together—the system. In many ways, I view my home as an organization, and I am functioning as the CLO (Chief Life Officer). I need to have good systems in place to ensure those who live there feel loved and valued and are learning the skills they need to live independent, happy, and successful lives.

  Define what being a "good mom" means to you based on what your personal circumstances and family needs are. After all, the only people who really matter and evaluate that definition are those who live in your home.

- **Personality styles**: We all have certain tendencies based on personality styles and approaches to communication that can impact decision-making. If you have natural tendencies that are more geared toward people-pleasing and are motivated to help others, that will likely contribute to how much you take on. If you avoid conflict in an effort to maintain relationships and prevent people from disliking you, then that can also contribute to putting the needs of others above your own, simply out of fear of damaging the relationship.

Don't get me wrong. These are wonderful attributes to have. But when your strengths are overused and you overextend yourself to the point that it causes burnout or stress, your tendency to constantly put others first can have a negative impact on your own well-being. This happens often without even realizing the impact until it has already taken its toll.

Reflecting on my past experiences and where I am today, what I have learned to prioritize is taking care of myself and developing stronger relationships with my children, rather than trying to control who they are and what they do. Needless to say, it has not been easy, particularly with a Type A personality style. My drive to get things done often came in the form of needing control of everything around me, causing me to add too much to my already-full plate.

These are daily practices I work on and am sure will be a life-long skill to hone. I have also learned that many leadership skills translate to the home and, I believe, help improve my parenting. The biggest leadership capability is developing my emotional intelligence, and throughout this book, I will further explain and incorporate those lessons so that you can benefit—as long as you put them into practice.

So, what does it take to operate differently and create the type of change *you* crave?

I believe that women can achieve what they want—and it's not about taking on more. You must know who you are to understand your own tendencies and how those tendencies impact your behavior and decisions. You also need to clearly define what you want and prioritize what is important. Then act accordingly.

If you want a life of purpose and meaning, you can't catch everything that is thrown your way. You need to identify the pitches that aren't worth catching and let them go, and practice throwing some back. Then, be prepared for a few bruises. You know there will be a few curveballs thrown your way.

To reach your ultimate potential and create the life you crave, you need to put in the hard and sometimes gut-wrenching work. Identify your strengths and limitations– what is *really* getting in your way of becoming who you want to be and getting what you want? That can be a painful process to go through—and requires a hard look at past decisions and behaviors. Many people don't like to admit their weaknesses. But when you can, and own them, you will be on a much healthier path to shedding that unwanted emotional weight. Some of the other hard work will come from dealing with change— not only how you are responding to it—but managing your response to others who don't like the change you are creating.

You can gain your own sustenance to be able to give generously to others without sacrificing your own needs and wants. It will require you to do things differently and reprioritize the things you say "yes" to.

I recognize that where you are on your motherhood journey may dictate your time and capacity to work on yourself. Be persistent. Move forward with grit and grace. You, my dear friend, are worth it.

Endnotes

[6] Katherine Schaeffer, "Key Facts about Moms in the U.S.," Pew Research Center, May 9, 2023, https://www.pewresearch.org/fact-tank/2019/05/08/facts-about-u-s-mothers/.

CHAPTER 3

The Cornerstone

REFLECT: WORKBOOK

*"When you know who you are and what you
stand for, you stand in wisdom."*
– Oprah Winfrey

Throughout my career and particularly in more recent years, I have coached people from all walks of life and helped them to achieve not only their professional goals but also their personal ones. I work with them to gain perspective, prioritize what is important to them, and help them build confidence in their decision-making, which allows them to elevate who they are in multiple areas of their lives. To do this, they must do the "work" to achieve their personal vision. What is often most difficult is overcoming both real and perceived barriers.

You can't easily turn off who you are when you get to work or go out in public, so my philosophy is coaching the "whole" person. You are the same person who rolls out of bed and puts on your clothes as you are at work or anywhere else. Unfortunately, so many people work hard to mask their true identities to "fit in" to cultural expectations, only to find in time that the stress they are feeling is because their values are misaligned with those of the organization, boss, team, and possibly the job they do. And sometimes, in the relationships they have with their partner.

If you can identify the strengths you possess and understand how they contribute to your success at home and work, then you can leverage them more effectively. It creates stronger alignment and congruence across the things you do. For example, if you are super organized and are good at creating structure at home, you will likely add value at work with those same skills.

If you can identify your development opportunities and understand how they hold you back from achieving your best self at home and work, it allows you to work toward your goals more efficiently because you aren't having to turn a part of yourself "on" or "off" when you change environments. An example here might be if you have the tendency to interrupt people when they are talking or tell others what to do, you may have an opportunity to listen more and not talk everyone's ear off all the time, considering other perspectives more. You can work to improve your active listening skills with your family at home, friends, and colleagues you work with. (I know this because it is something I have had to work on over the years!) Doing so provides more opportunities to practice developing new habits regardless of your environment, which will increase your effectiveness.

Establishing Your Identity

In the early days of becoming a new mom—when I was married and working full time—I would take my daughter to playgroups, which allowed me to meet other moms. Through introductions and small talk, we would exchange the basic pleasantries of family life, sharing if we were married, how many other kids we had, and whether we had careers outside the home. After describing my work, I would often hear other moms who were stay-at-home parents describe themselves as, "Oh, I'm *just* a mom!"

Now, I am sure this was not intentional but I want to point out something about making this statement for any of you who may have allowed those words to come across your very own lips. For starters, you are not *just* a mom. You, my dear friend, are a strong, caring, reliable, resourceful woman who gets shit done. Many of you have not only given life to your children, but in many ways, you have sacrificed your own lives for them.

Yet, 88% of women surveyed indicated that being a mom is a key part of their personal identity, while 35% said it was the most important part of their identity (Pew Research 2023).[6]

I imagine that for some of you, being a mom feels like the only reason you exist, and I respect that. And there is so much more to who you are. But it is up to you to figure out who is underneath the lifelong assignment you have been given.

This often comes into play as you look at status and hierarchy in the workplace. Some of you may feel less worthy because you aren't a director or vice president—or at whatever level you think reflects your value. Some of you may be unemployed right now and struggling to find work. Whatever your situation, these lived experiences can impact your self-esteem.

Other factors may contribute to how you view your identity, such as who you are married to (or if you are married), the brand of shoes you wear, where you live, your title, and what car you drive. For some, your identity may be tied to a life of perfection that requires everything to be just right, including every pillow on the couch having a clean, crisp dent down the middle, as shown in home magazines.

Unfortunately, all of these things can be taken away at any time. None of us are guaranteed everything we want in life. Certainly, what we have in our possession now likely won't last a lifetime. If your identity is dependent on these external things, then you may actually be running further away from who you really are. Worse, you may be missing out on your true potential because you are tethered to the belief that it is only these things that will bring you joy and happiness in life.

When I begin working with clients, we explore their personal values and what they feel defines significance in their lives. The themes that commonly emerge for women are related to having a better sense of self, more confidence, and the ability to do something bigger. Never, ever, do I hear about wanting to get more things. It is about wanting to become more of who they are and having a positive impact on those around them.

Another common theme I hear is about the importance of family. People often describe a desire to achieve things that are important to *them*. Notice how those themes can be diametrically opposing. For moms, how can you prioritize family, contribute to the greater good, *and* prioritize yourself? You can start by ensuring that you are on your list of priorities and knowing what *you* value. If you don't demonstrate to others that you value yourself, you are essentially teaching them not to value you as well. If you don't elevate yourself, who will?

With my second pregnancy, I had to step back and reflect on who I was and what was most important in my life. It allowed me the ability to consider what I valued, what I stood for, and what I needed to not only survive, but thrive. I realized that I needed to slow down and be more intentional with my choices. I also had to remind myself that I was the master of figuring things out and would make it through somehow. One day at a time.

We all have struggles and are more alike than we probably realize. I suspect you want to not only survive each day but actually thrive. You may want a stronger sense of belonging and acceptance. A place where you can truly be yourself, express your thoughts openly, be heard without being judged, and get the support you need when you are in the throes of a storm, just trying to get by until the clouds pass.

We all are unique in who we are, what we do, and how we impact the world around us. My question is, *"Who are you, and what do you stand for?"* When you strip away the roles you fill of mom, partner, sister, daughter, colleague, etc., who are you? What makes you, *you*?

In the day-to-day grind of work, kids, appointments, family issues, drama with friends, health issues, etc., it is easy to get caught up running on the proverbial hamster wheel—going from one thing to the next, barely breathing. It is this operating mode that contributes to the overwhelm, burnout, and lack of satisfaction. Furthermore, you likely don't even know how you are feeling, because you aren't slowing down long enough to assess what that looks like. Often, all that energy is being placed on everyone and everything but yourself. At times, the things on your plate don't align with your values, what you want for yourself, or the type of relationships you desire to have. Worse yet—the people around you likely see it and feel it too.

I have provided some questions below so you can start to reflect. If you want to create change in your life and achieve your highest potential, take time to reflect and understand more about who you are. It is from there that you will establish a solid foundation to further build upon.

As I alluded to earlier, throughout this book, I will provide you with some prompts to reflect and gain insight into your own personal experiences and identify the goals you have for yourself. An important starting point is seeking answers to some foundational questions.

In a journal or in the spaces provided on the next few pages, read through the questions and begin to explore answers by writing them down—putting pen to paper. There is no right or wrong, good or bad response. Just answer based on what you truly feel and what comes to mind without editing your thoughts. The key takeaway here is to gain insight into who you are and understand the core values from which you want to operate in life.

This will be important information for you to come back to as you complete additional exercises in later chapters.

What is currently on your plate? If you were to write down the responsibilities you have across work, home, and family, what would your plate look like? This is an opportunity to take inventory of how you currently spend your time.

_____

_____

_____

_____

_____

_____

_____

_____

_____

_____

_____

_____

_____

_____

_____

_____

_____

_____

What do you value in life? Reflect on what drives your behaviors and decisions. Be sure to identify what *your* values are rather than what others may want or expect. For example, you might value things like family, faith, financial freedom, status, creativity, or autonomy.

What are your core beliefs? How would you describe your belief system? Consider beliefs you have about yourself, other people, or the world in general. For example, a belief you may have about yourself might be, "Being a mom is my most important role in life."

Are there false beliefs that you have come to believe over time? These could be based on what you have heard from others or have misinterpreted. For example, "I must do everything myself."

_____

_____

_____

_____

_____

_____

_____

_____

_____

_____

_____

_____

_____

_____

_____

_____

_____

_____

Where are you out of alignment with your values and beliefs?
Where are you operating outside of your values or in ways that are incongruent with what is important to you? What beliefs do you need to rewrite to create the change you want?

Reflect on what you wrote down previously when you described what is on your plate. Below, write down areas in which you may feel out of alignment with what you value. This will help you identify potential areas to make changes.

_____

_____

_____

_____

_____

_____

_____

_____

_____

_____

_____

_____

_____

_____

Asking yourself the previous questions is just the start. Truly trans-forming yourself will require you to take an honest look at where you are and where you want to go and identify strategies to move you in that direction. It will also require that you learn to work through the challenges that will come your way—*with the expectation that you will make it through to the other side*. It may not happen exactly as you had hoped, and it may not happen exactly when you want it, but you will move closer to the life you crave.

Are you ready to elevate yourselves, moms?

Endnotes

(6)   Katherine Schaeffer, "Key Facts about Moms in the U.S.," Pew Research Center, May 9, 2023, https://www.pewresearch.org/fact-tank/2019/05/08/facts-about-u-s-mothers/.

KEY TAKEAWAYS

Principle #1: Reflection is the key to self-preservation.

1. Hit the pause button to step back and figure out what is on your plate.

2. Consider how you are feeling so you can process those feelings effectively.

3. Reflect on your values and where your true priorities lie.

4. Identify where you are operating out of alignment with your values or where you want to spend more time.

5. Ground yourself in those values and what you believe to have confidence and conviction when you make decisions.

PRINCIPLE #2

Rediscovering possibilities is essential to feeding your soul

CHAPTER 4

Glass Half-Full

"Find out who you are and do it on purpose."
– Dolly Parton

Probably like you, I had it "all" planned out when I was in my early twenties—maybe even earlier.

- ✓ Step 1: Graduate from college.
- ✓ Step 2: Meet the man of my dreams.
- ✓ Step 3: Get married.
- ✓ Step 4: Have three kids.
- ✓ Step 5: Live happily ever after.

I expected the steps to occur in that order. I wasn't so concerned with where my career fell because, in my mind, my life would *start* when I got married and had kids. I anticipated these events to occur as if I would simply check them off a to-do list that I created on a Post-it note and stuck to my refrigerator. As if they were some tasks I would easily complete—all by the ripe old age of twenty-seven. That was *my* plan, so to speak.

Little did I realize, the beginning of my life as a mother would start before my kids were even born. I met my ex-husband at the

Jersey Shore; he had just moved from Philadelphia to Boston, and I was living in New Jersey. We dated long-distance for a good portion of our relationship—but not before relocating multiple times. He ended up taking a job in northern California, which obviously put a wrench in my plan because I had a feeling he was "the one". After all, I had surpassed the age of twenty-seven by then, which was the age at which I planned to be married and start a family.

I was unsure about moving all the way across the country, especially not being engaged at the time. I remember him telling me, "I just want to do this for a couple of years." He had a great career and was advancing in his profession, making great money. While I was successful in my career, I had just completed my graduate degree in Organizational Management. To help others understand what that is in simpler terms, it involves helping organizations to improve performance through systems of planning, measuring, monitoring, and providing feedback to achieve results. It is deeply tied to leading organizational change and requires a good understanding of what it takes to get a lot of people rowing in the same direction.

I wasn't sure if I wanted to spend the rest of my life in New Jersey. So, I did what many young women have done and accommodated my then-partner by moving across the country to be near him. But instead of moving in with him, I moved to southern California with a friend from graduate school. Our location of choice? Carlsbad.

He eventually relocated to southern California, where I was living, and a few years later we got married and had our daughter, Brooke. By then, I was excelling in my own career, but as a newly married person, I still felt like I was following my husband and his dreams, sidelining all the things I had dreamt of for myself.

Following his career felt like the right thing to do once we were married and had our daughter. That is what seemed to be the "norm". He was successful, made great money—a lot more than me—and we were in love. But I never really asked myself what *I* wanted. I was expecting my life to unfold much like I had seen in all of the movies and fairytales.

For many years to come, I continued hearing him say, "...just a couple more years...", as if at the end of those years, he would be satisfied with his accomplishments. The problem was his target kept changing, and I became complacent. I soon realized his dreams would always take precedence over mine.

I set aside what I wanted to make him happy and be a good mom, all while ignoring my inner voice. On the surface, it appeared I was getting something better by following him. After all, we had a great life by most standards. We lived in southern California, had a beautiful home, a great social life, great friends, and the means to buy just about anything we desired. But in hindsight, I realized that suppressing my own desires made way for feelings of resentment— not just toward him, but toward myself. After we got divorced and I became pregnant a second time, I finally asked myself, "What do you want?"

CHAPTER 5

Untapped Potential

"Our only limitations are those we set up in our own minds."
– Napoleon Hill

Many times, we close ourselves off to what "could be" because we are so focused on what we think will keep us from getting what we want. Or worse, we fail to define what we want, resulting in our lives simply unfolding in front of us, with no direction. Reacting to situations and feeling stuck.

To create the change you want in life, you have to aim for something—some sort of target that will help you reach your potential. You may be afraid to think too big and extend your reach because of what you believe success will bring, or you just never take the time to sit and think about what *you* want, regardless of what everyone says you *should* want.

Then there are all other ways people, especially moms, hold themselves back. As in my case, I surrendered to the fairytale story in my mind about how my life was supposed to unfold. You get married, the husband works and provides for the family, and the wife stays home to raise the kids. Period. But what happens in fairytales when the couple gets divorced, and the mom gets pregnant again?

Oh, yeah. They don't write about those stories—that is why I'm here to share mine with you.

You will read more about this in later chapters, but we will begin to explore the topic of barriers at a high level here. We limit ourselves by being suckered into:

- Unworthiness
- Imposter syndrome
- Not wanting to surpass the success of others (i.e., partner, siblings, friends, or peers)
- Fear of judgment
- Fear of how others will perceive us

This is a short list of the feelings and beliefs you may let permeate your mind and hold you back from living your best life. I say this with certainty because I have seen what women can do when they unlock their potential. They follow their passions and put plans in place to achieve the visions they have for themselves. I have seen the look in their eyes change and the confidence return when they follow their intuition, listen to that voice inside, and go after what they have been yearning for...even when they didn't believe they had the ability. I have also experienced it myself—and I would be a fool to think those thoughts won't cross my mind again. But now I know better. Passions and intuition are gifts, and they have been given uniquely to you in the way you have received them...perfectly on time.

This is the magic in life because we have the opportunity to make decisions based on who we are uniquely and individually. I encourage you to be intentional about your life choices, instead of surrendering to life's circumstances, other people, and fate. You have so much more agency over your life than you may be giving yourself credit for.

When I finally asked myself, "What do I want?" following my second pregnancy, I took some time to explore what could be. I had options. Some were better than others. But the one thing I started with was focusing on what I wanted and needed, rather than what others wanted. I also stopped worrying about how others would respond to my desires. As I reflect on the primary issues I was trying to solve, it was about adjusting my finances to ensure I could provide for my family and surrounding myself with the support I knew I would so desperately need.

When I say "support", this could be described in several different ways. For one, I needed emotional support. That required me to be around people I trusted and loved, and who loved me unconditionally—people who were going to cheer me on when I would be hanging on by a thread. Two, I would need physical help. Having a second child on my own would mean I would have to be on call 24/7 every day of the year. With a newborn, that can be exhausting, to say the least. Have you ever been so sick yourself, and still needed to take care of a newborn or toddler? It is nearly impossible. I say nearly because I did it and made it through. I'm sure many of you have too. I knew that I needed to be around people who were willing to step in to help so I could take time to recharge—even if it was only for fifteen minutes.

There were a couple of things I considered as I contemplated the possibilities of what to do next:

> **Option 1**: Stay in the home I was living in, in southern California, and adjust my finances accordingly. I could try to find a higher-paying job or take on a second job.

> **Option 2**: Stay in southern California but move into a smaller place and rent to minimize

expenses. I could still consider finding a new job or taking on a second job.

Option 3: Move closer to family on the east coast, cut costs all together, and be around people who could help me out as a single parent to two kids.

There were other options to consider, but overall, those were the big decisions I had to make. As I thought about my situation and the fact that my mom was being treated for cancer, I chose option three. Out of the options I mentioned, it was the hardest one of all, and it was going to upset many people in the process. Yet, I had to reconfigure my priorities in life and make some difficult decisions to get to the place I wanted to be—decisions that other people weren't going to like, or maybe even support.

Despite the fear of the unknown that I felt, deep down there was a glimmer of hope and excitement about what was yet to come for me in life. I knew there were a lot of possibilities available to consider and looked at them strategically. It was like trying to piece together my future as if it were a puzzle that sat in front of me in a thousand different pieces. As I think back to those moments, feeling a roller-coaster of emotions, I realize I was becoming more grounded in who I wanted to be. I was sticking to my values and what was important to me—putting my family first, taking calculated risks, being creative, asserting my independence, and having faith in the unknown—but always believing things would work out. I also wanted peace in my life. I had a yearning to slow down, breathe, and take in the world around me. Even if things didn't turn out the way I had conjured up in my mind, I knew things would be okay. *We* would be okay. But the hard work was yet to come.

Exploring Possibilities

To identify where you want to go, you must open your mind to all of the things you ever wanted, even the dream shots—do not constrain yourself. Our minds are powerful tools, so if you can take time to visualize what you want in your future, it can be a great motivator and compass.

Many people limit their beliefs. If they want to switch careers, they think about how hard it would be and how they will never get a job in a new field. Or, if they dream about advancing in their organization, they focus on the politics, the people they are competing with, or everything they have on their plate, and assume they can't take on more and give up. If they dream of stepping back from their careers to stay at home more or work less, they worry about the conversations they must have with bosses and family and what it might mean five years from now when they reenter the workforce. But if they never take the jump, they'll just spend five more years not enjoying work or life.

Limiting your beliefs or focusing on negative thoughts creates a stress response in your body. This is also known as the "fight-or-flight" response, which is caused by the activation of the sympathetic nervous system. When felt, you might experience an increase in heart rate, flushed skin, or an increase in blood pressure. Sometimes it is all of those things! It is your body's response to a perceived threat.

It would be naïve to believe that working toward your dreams comes without any barriers or sacrifices. However, allowing yourself to consider a future based on what you want for yourself is one of the most empowering and liberating things you can do. When you shift your thoughts to what is possible, your body can begin the shift from "fight-or-flight" to rest and repair, which is much better for your immune system and your overall physical and mental health.

Time is one of the most valuable resources we have, and yet, so many people I know don't take time to reflect on or dream about what they want.

Have you been adding things to your plate that align with who you are and what you want, or are you filling it with perceived priorities or distractions that are ultimately keeping you from what you *really* desire?

CHAPTER 6

Elevate Yourself

REDISCOVER: WORKBOOK

*"Create the highest, grandest vision possible for your
life because you become what you believe."*
– Oprah Winfrey

Throughout my career and personal life, I have had the pleasure of getting to know many moms. Some are stay-at-home moms, and others have careers and jobs working outside of the home. I hear them describe success differently, yet common themes have emerged around the barriers many experience in achieving success, which include:

- prioritizing everyone and everything else above their own needs
- focusing on obstacles—whether they are real or perceived
- failing to be clear about what they want
- unwillingness to put in the work to create the change they desire
- not having the support system needed to sustain the change

The primary thing I see is people not taking time to step back and reflect on what is truly important to them. Many of the women I have coached, and even friends and family with whom I have spoken, rarely take time to step back and explore what they want for themselves. In the past, they may have dreamt about achieving certain things in life. But with all the life responsibilities that tend to fall on moms, few think about themselves, if at all. They struggle to see themselves as individuals and what is important to them outside of the role of a mom, partner, career person, friend, etc.

Most of these women want to focus on their personal life priorities and contribute at home and work in meaningful ways. They want to feel good about how they spend their time so that it is fulfilling and to achieve the dreams they have for themselves—this is self-care at its best. Yet, achieving what they want is often put on the back burner or is perceived to be out of reach.

Over the years I have developed programs to help people develop their capabilities and create the change they are seeking. Most often this is in a work setting. More recently, I created a program specifically for working moms to help them prioritize themselves and invest in their futures according to what *they* wanted. No surprise, the stresses of the home are often just as intense or more so than the stresses of the workplace.

So, I am sharing with you some of the tools I have used with clients to help you get a head start. You will start by opening your mind to possibilities and capturing your ideas—without limiting yourself. In the previous section, I encouraged you to explore some questions, which I want you to reflect on. What themes begin to emerge as you look at the list you created? What clarity did you gain about what is important to you?

I suspect some of you may identify with the desire to prioritize yourself and allow for more time for self-care. A manicure or a massage every month is a start, but I suspect it isn't going to create the sustained change you are seeking. It's also not about checking off items from your to-do list.

What I'm asking you to do is prioritize things that are important to *you* to create and sustain the life you choose for yourself. It's just like placing that oxygen mask on yourself first. When you board a plane and get ready to take off, there is a reason the flight crew announces, *"Place the oxygen mask on yourself before attending to small children or others that may need your assistance."* If you don't take care of yourself, you won't be able to give anything to others at home or work—certainly not the best of you. In the end, it is about ensuring you stay on the priority list and aren't always serving others first.

I know. That will feel uncomfortable. You might be thinking, what will others say about me if I put myself first? Will they think I'm a "bad mom"? Honestly, it is a possibility. However, others don't have the context you do, and only you can determine what is best for you—no one else. Or maybe guilt is creeping in, and you can't bear to put yourself first. Well, my friend…how's that working out for you?

Only you can create the change you want for yourself. We will explore how to overcome some of the barriers you are likely considering, or even experiencing, later. For now, I want you to consider your "ask". What do *you* want?

Grab a pen and go sit in a quiet place (even if it means going in the bathroom and locking the door for ten minutes so you can have some alone time…which I'm not ashamed to say I have done from time to time…assuming you can do so without anyone getting harmed in the process!). Review the questions on the next few pages so you can identify where you want to go. Remember…no limits!

What is the vision you have for yourself? Describe words that characterize who you strive to be, which includes some of the positive traits you have now. Who do you want to become? List your ideas below.

List twenty things you want to do in life. Consider the images you have had in your mind of what you wanted (and still want) for yourself. If you need a starting point, start listing things you have always wanted to do. Remember, focus on possibilities, not obstacles.

Now that you have identified possibilities, review what you wrote down and see if any themes emerge. Maybe your themes revolve around being more creative or providing yourself with the opportunity for freedom of self-expression, or maybe they reflect your desire to have more agency in life. There is no right or wrong. This exercise is unique to you and where you want to be in the future—as of today. Whatever the themes may be, keep them close by. Tape them to your closet door, mount them on your car dash, and put them in the Notes app on your phone. Read them daily. You will refer to this information in later chapters.

After you have considered some of these questions, it can help to surround yourself with the things (and people) that will support you on your path. Create a vision board. Find a mentor you trust to be your accountability partner. Set up a structured time to talk, plan, and discuss your thoughts as you begin your new pathway. Keeping your vision visible is an important reminder of what you want for yourself (and why it's important) and can also be a great motivator to witness your progress.

KEY TAKEAWAYS

Principle #2: Rediscovering possibilities is essential to feeding your soul.

1. Explore all the possibilities that exist to open your mind up to other solutions.

2. When you focus on barriers, reframe your thinking to opportunities that exist.

3. Pay attention to what you are feeling as you explore possibilities. Joy awaits.

4. Choose wisely and move forward with intention.

5. Be clear to yourself and others about what you want.

PRINCIPLE #3

It's never too late to reset priorities based on what is important to you.

CHAPTER 7

Starting Anew

*"Self-care is giving the world the best of
you instead of what's left of you."*
– Katie Reed

I can remember the place, the entire conversation, and the response I received when telling my boss that I would be quitting my job and moving to Ohio. It was around the holidays, and we had a tradition of going out for cocktails along with another colleague and friend. These were some of the most memorable times I had with them. My boss was one of the best mentors I've ever had—and we remain close to this day. But at the time, I worked closely with her and knew how much she trusted me—it was a relationship most people would envy. I worried she would feel like I was quitting *her.* She had provided me with so many wonderful opportunities throughout my career and had seen potential in me that, on many days, evaded my very own thoughts and beliefs. I knew this conversation wasn't going to be easy. And boy, was I right!

We all met at a swanky restaurant in Newport Beach, California. We sat down in the busy bar area at a high-top table, exchanged our hellos, and got updates from each other on general work and life stuff. We talked about family and our plans for Christmas. But I knew I wouldn't be able to keep my secret much longer. One of the first signs that something wasn't right was when I didn't order a martini—specifically a Cosmo—which was our signature drink when we all got together. I got a strange look from both of them when I ordered water with lemon. This was my opportunity.

I didn't beat around the bush. I jumped right in to say that I was pregnant and given my situation, which also included my mom being treated for cancer, I had made the decision to move back east. I think my boss may have thought I was kidding at first, but I will never forget the look on her face as the smile wore off. She may have initially thought, and even said, "You're kidding, right?" She quickly realized I wasn't.

Though I don't recall the exact words she said, I know I felt defensive because that was my typical conflict response. But this time was different. To put this into perspective, I was fully aware that my leaving the company was going to be difficult for my boss, given the knowledge I had and the work I was doing, but I also knew that everyone is replaceable. Sad, but true. My leaving wasn't going to be the end of the world, though I suspect she felt that way at the time.

I remember hearing her sharing things that were, I believe, intended to help me consider all perspectives. Yet, it felt like she was saying to me, "I don't agree with your decision. You should reconsider staying." There is that word. "Should". Maybe she didn't say those words exactly, but that is what I heard. It was at that moment that I knew I had made the right decision...for me.

So often we allow others to influence our decisions in life. Many times, it is because we don't want to disappoint them, especially our family, boss, or close friends. What my boss didn't realize was that I had already done the internal work of thinking through every detail of the change that lay ahead for me. What I valued—and still value today—was driving my decision. It was about exploring the unknown, taking risks, and problem-solving, but also about being closer to family, being grounded in my community, and having a support system. It is those things that help me feel confident in my ability to be successful both personally and professionally. At my core, I knew I needed to leave California. It wasn't just about surviving; I wanted to thrive as a single parent to two kids. It was the most confident decision I think I've ever made—even though it meant I would disappoint others, especially my boss.

In the end, she understood my decision and was fully supportive. I agreed to stay on and work remotely until they hired a replacement. Then, I helped train that person remotely.

It all worked out just the way it was supposed to, but that doesn't mean it didn't come with some difficulties. In the span of three months, after learning I was pregnant, I sold my house in California, bought one in Ohio, packed up my daughter and dog, and drove across the country—close to five months pregnant. I continued working until about April of the following year and then took some time off until Parker was born in June. My mom passed away that October. I can remember her last visit to Ohio to spend time with my sister and me. Mom was able to meet Parker, and though he was only about four months old when she passed, I'm grateful she got to hold him. I'm pretty sure that is the only photo I have of the two of them together. That is one picture I'm grateful for.

A meaningful life is about the value we create for ourselves and others. What I have learned is that success is specific and unique to each person. How a stay-at-home mom defines her priorities and views success will likely differ from how a full-time working mom who is an executive at a large company views it. Your success in life is not dictated by what others do or what they think about what you do; it is determined by how you measure success, execute your plan, and measure your results.

What often gets in the way is the pressure of what other people believe is best for you, causing you to question if it is what you want.

Or sometimes it is simply to appease others. It is important to note that everyone has their own life experiences, beliefs, and views of the world through their eyes. While other perspectives are great to hear, and can certainly be considered, make no mistake—they are biased. If you find yourself accommodating the needs of others too often, you may end up with too much on your plate, and worse, not achieving what is important to you.

Success doesn't always come with the number of things you can get done or the dollars flowing into your bank account. When it is your time to leave this earth, those likely won't be what you will reflect on. My guess is you will be focused on doing the things you wish you had prioritized earlier—or celebrating all of the things you did do. I certainly learned that as I watched my mom in her final days, and I know she lived a life of meaning.

A Client Story of Resetting Priorities

Months passed with us spending hours discussing what she wanted in her next career move. "I know what I don't want," she said.

She was a coaching client of mine who had a vision in her mind of what that next role would be like but struggled to define what it would take to obtain it and how she would measure success. We often discussed whether she was running away from her current role or genuinely running toward something bigger and better. It would be difficult to achieve her vision and run toward something if she was not clear about what success looked like in her next role.

I kept bringing her back to her vision and identifying her non-negotiables—title, location, company size, number of direct reports, role responsibilities, etc. We spent time talking through those details, discussing her strengths and the contributions she could make, and where she wanted to stretch herself and learn more, which in her current role wasn't being fulfilled. It was only after she gained clarity around those things that she could begin identifying the right opportunities to pursue and put her energy into, versus taking interviews with organizations that didn't align with what she truly wanted. Once she hit the reset button and claimed what she wanted, her dream job finally came across her path. She recognized that it was necessary to take her time and really define what success looked like—and then be persistent...and patient through the process. In one of our recent coaching sessions, she said, "I have found my dream job and I'm so glad I waited. I finally feel like I found the right opportunity and I'm achieving my vision."

I am happy to report that my client is still in that role and is thriving. She is transformed in a way I don't think either of us expected—she is in her element and seems more content. Her vision became a reality because she got crystal clear on the things she needed to do to achieve her vision—and then got to work.

CHAPTER 8

Speak Up

"The first step to getting what you want is having the courage to get rid of what you don't."
– Unknown

So many times, we pile more on top of our plate because of things other people want, then, we accept the leftovers—if there are any. Worse, we fail to take things off our plate to make room for something new. It is time to reset priorities based on what is important to *you*—not others. Now, I realize some of you are likely married and have partners or have other people in your lives who are impacted by your decisions. I get that. What I would ask you to consider is whether you have placed your dreams and desires on a shelf because you don't believe people would support them. Or maybe people in your life have communicated that they don't support your dreams and you have succumbed to the belief it isn't worth the fight. Please listen: *Liberate yourself. You are worth it.*

Prioritizing what is important to you can be achieved in small steps each day. As I mentioned earlier, this book isn't about just setting aside an hour to go do something for yourself, like getting your nails or hair done or having a massage. It is about consistently taking those steps that begin a new habit. Doing things for yourself and feeling good as a result improves your outlook on life. It increases your confidence. Even if the feelings are only temporary, you begin to realize that prioritizing yourself is a good thing for you and, ultimately, others. You just have to get through the hard parts of having the conversation, and then sometimes deal with the resistance from people around you.

When I decided to quit my job in California and move to Ohio, I knew that I would need to have some tough conversations, particularly with my boss and my ex-husband, as both would view the change as pretty significant.

For my boss, there were some key things I anticipated she would worry about, given my decision:

- Existing projects I was working on
- Future goals we had established for the year
- Loss of historical business knowledge and established relationships
- Cost of replacement…

…the list goes on. So, I did what I do best, and sat down to strategize. I thought about the concerns she would have and identified a few options to propose to her to help minimize the impact on her, the team, and the business. This demonstrated empathy for her situation and took some of the burden off her shoulders. In the end, we landed on a couple of key things I recall, including:

- Identifying existing projects and completing what I could, as well as developing a transition plan for anything that would need to be done beyond my last day.
- Drafting a transition plan and reviewing it with her to get input and align actions.

- Preparing a communication plan, which meant I had to wait to share my news with anyone until she had time to discuss the situation with the CEO.
- Probably most importantly, I agreed to work remotely after my move, to help with transitioning the work, and offered to help onboard the new person.

By doing these things, I helped my boss feel confident about the work getting done and allowed her to spend time ensuring things were done in the best way possible with the least impact on the business. I have enjoyed my working career in industry and have had wonderful opportunities to grow but let me be clear about one thing: everyone is replaceable. I mean that with all the love in my heart. For anyone who thinks they aren't, you are fooling yourself. Now, I'm not suggesting that every organization is out to suck the life out of their employees—even though some do. There are many wonderful employers out there, and when you think about how you can make your boss's life easier and help the business out, they are generally more likely going to help you too. So, that is what I did.

I thought having the conversation with my ex-husband was a crapshoot. I needed to tell him that I was pregnant (not that he would care) and that I was moving our daughter two thousand miles across the country…in about three months. So, what did I do? I, again, sat down to strategize and considered how to best influence him, while maintaining the relationship. This was going to be a tough one. It was a conversation I was dreading.

I remember the day I called him. I was sitting in my office at work, working on projects and trying to get things organized before leaving. I felt ready—I was in execution mode and figured I would call while I was feeling confident. I had thought about what I wanted to say and anticipated how he might react.

He had bought a house not far from where Brooke and I lived. I knew he was settled in and happy with his life. I figured he would have to agree that I had put a lot of my goals and dreams in life on hold for him…having moved across the country from New Jersey to California for him; having agreed to stay at home with Brooke while he continued to work. He was constantly on the road for his job, so I essentially operated like a single mom. Not that he wasn't a good dad—he was, but he wasn't always around. The time he spent with her often involved the fun stuff, while I was the one at home taking care of her, the house, and everything else that keeps a family afloat. I also recognized what was important to him: he saw himself as the provider for the family. That is how he was raised—and he has always done a wonderful job in doing so. For that, I am forever grateful. He provided a wonderful life in California, and even to this day, I know I can depend on him. But I knew the conversation would be difficult and that he could very easily tell me to go to hell.

When he picked up the phone, I could feel my heart beating out of my chest. I had to remind myself to stay calm, not just for me but to ensure the conversation went smoothly—he often shut down when I got emotional. More importantly, I wanted to make sure I managed my emotions to minimize the stress my body might experience. I wanted to keep my baby safe. Unnecessary stress isn't good for any mom. Boy, was I under a lot of stress.

I didn't waste much time. "Hi. I have something important to talk to you about, so I need your undivided attention. Do you have fifteen minutes or so?" He was infamous for not talking long on the phone. He would often cut you off, saying, "I gotta go." It was often—almost always—related to his work. So, when he heard me say those words, I could tell he was listening.

"As you know, my mom is being treated for cancer back in New York. It has been difficult dealing with this, and I want to spend more time with her. Plus, I'm pregnant."

He didn't hesitate. "What? You're pregnant? What...?"

I cut him off. "I don't want to get into the details. What I will tell you is that I'm doing this on my own, and I need to get back east to be near my family. I have basically followed you around for years, and now it's my turn. I'm asking for your support."

I told him that I understood this was shocking news, and that it wasn't going to be easy, but I made it clear—with conviction—that I had a plan, and it was really important for me to carry it through.

"I understand, Kathy. Whatever you need, I will support you," he said. My jaw hit the floor. I had never felt so much compassion and warmth come from him as I did in that moment. I felt supported and, in a way, free. I was finally going to prioritize myself. The power dynamic had shifted.

In previous chapters, we explored what is important to you, identified who you want to become, and looked at possibilities. Now, it is about defining what you really want and gaining clarity on the direction you want to go.

Even when you know what you want, the path to get there isn't always straightforward. It's not easy to figure out the "*how*" on your own. When you don't have clarity around what you want, you run the risk of spending time on things that aren't aligned with your values, your vision, or what your true priorities are. The result? You add more to your plate than is necessary. When you have clarity about what you want, you increase the likelihood of staying in alignment.

I could have stayed in California and gone with a backup plan, so to speak. But I would not have the peace I now have. That, my friends, is priceless.

While some of you may be setting goals for the first time, I suspect the vast majority of you aren't new to this practice. And since goals can change over time, I'm suggesting you hit "reset". Prioritize where you are spending your time, energy, and focus. It may be relatively easy to establish a plan, but it will also require mental toughness and developing new behaviors and habits as you move forward. You will inevitably be met with obstacles and situations that will pull you back into your comfort zone. But remember, we don't experience growth in life without some level of discomfort.

Just as I experienced, you too will have situations and people who will create obstacles to achieving your goals, so much so that you may feel defeated and even give up. That is where grit and grace come in. As you work to hit the reset button and realign your priorities, you are going to be faced with situations that will get the best of you and bring out the worst in you—whether that is other people resisting your new ways of doing things, getting in your own way by ruminating on negative thoughts, or resorting to habits that weren't serving you well in the first place.

Grit is about perseverance over the long haul. It's about knowing where you are going and staying the course—through the highest triumphs and the lowest valleys. It is about identifying those negative thoughts that go through your head when you experience setbacks, and reframing your thinking, whether that is reminding yourself of why you are doing it, thinking about how you'll feel when you get to where you want to go, or simply saying to yourself, "This too shall pass and tomorrow is a new day." Perseverance is not easy to develop—but when you have a clear vision and determination, it can be worth the temporary discomfort.

While grit is important to stay the course, you will also need to show yourself some kindness in the process, which in my opinion, is all about grace. Grace is having favor, showing compassion, and giving leniency. It's not easy to give yourself grace, especially when you are questioning your own decisions. It can be even harder to give grace to others. Yet, everyone needs it, and amazing things can happen when it is granted.

It amazes me sometimes to hear the things women say to themselves. I, too, have fallen into the spiral of negative self-talk. We can say things internally that are deeply damaging to our well-being. If your best friend were to criticize herself the way you do yourself, would you allow that, or would you intervene?

Grit and grace are necessary to help you achieve your vision. This also requires a more granular look into the day-to-day activities and actions you will need to accomplish to achieve your vision. It will also require you to anticipate potential roadblocks. This is the one area of life-changing action that is often overlooked.

Part of the excitement and joy I get from life is when I'm thrown a curveball. Now, I realize I have the choice to swing as hard as I can to knock it out of the park, or I can choose to let someone else catch it because it wasn't worth the energy of my swing.

CHAPTER 9

Gaining Clarity

RESET: WORKBOOK

"The most difficult thing is the decision to act,
the rest is merely tenacity."
– Amelia Earhart

The coaching client I had been working with finally gained clarity about what she wanted. She established specific objectives and narrowed down her focus as she explored new opportunities. Today, she is in a Vice President role at a well-established organization and is extremely happy. She has a great working relationship with her boss and can leverage her strengths. It was because of the time she took to get clear on what she wanted that she was able to achieve her vision. She also demonstrated a lot of grit in the process as she waited for the right opportunity to come along.

In the process of deciding to move back east following my pregnancy and Mom's cancer diagnosis, I had to get crystal clear on what I needed and wanted. But to achieve it, I had to prepare for several difficult conversations with my sister, my ex-husband, and my boss… conversations that I dreaded, but knew if I didn't have them, I would be holding myself back from the life I was trying to create—a life where I could thrive. As difficult as they were, I'm glad I took those risks.

Some other key "ingredients" may also be necessary once you have defined your priorities and will help you along the way as you work to fulfill your vision.

- **Make your desires known.** There is something about stating what you want out loud, telling others, and writing it down. It helps bring your goals to life—and in a way, sends the message out to the universe regarding your intention. It elevates the law of attraction, which states that we attract into our lives whatever we are focused on. If you focus on positive thoughts and have goals you aim to achieve, you will find a way to achieve them.

- **Be disciplined.** Be consistent in working toward what you want to achieve, which may require you to demonstrate new behaviors and do things that will help you produce the desired outcomes. This is about true self-accountability. It's doing what you know you need, and want to do for yourself, even when no one else is there to remind you.

- **Establish a support system.** Being disciplined is essential, but it helps to have a support system. An accountability partner can be one of the best ways to achieve your goals. This could be a friend, a family member, or a coach to provide positive reinforcement and constructive feedback to keep you on the right track. Recognize that you also need to be willing to listen to feedback from others. This might mean working with someone who thinks differently from you, so you can gain new perspectives, or someone who will push you to drive results. Choose wisely.

- **Stay flexible.** Despite having an action plan and knowing what it will take to achieve your vision, things don't always turn out as you had hoped. Because of this, it is essential to remain flexible about what life brings. Stay open and know that you can still reach your goals, although it may require you to take a different road than the one you had envisioned. In some cases, you may end up at a place that was actually better than you originally planned. In those unexpected twists and turns, you may find beauty in things or learn something along the way.

- **Keep a good attitude *and* sense of humor.** It doesn't matter what you are trying to achieve in life; you are bound to come across situations that are going to be frustrating. You can either sulk and let those situations bring you down—taking you further from where you want to go—or you can get right back up when you fall, brush yourself off, and move on.

- **Be clear about what you need from others—and be ready to negotiate.** There are likely others from whom you need help to achieve your vision, whether that is your partner, child(ren), boss, or friend(s). When you can clearly articulate what you need, people are more likely to understand their role in helping you.

- **Take time to reflect on your progress.** Take time to sit back and reflect on how far you have come. It is easy to get stuck in reactive mode, moving from one thing to the next. It's not until you take time to think about where you came from, where you are today, and where you want to go—that you identify the progress you have made. It is also an opportunity to identify any adjustments that may be required to help you move forward more effectively. This can be done by journaling, connecting with your coach or accountability partner, or just taking time to reflect on your own. Set an intention for what is needed to continue making progress and be sure to celebrate your wins, no matter how insignificant they may seem. Progress can be a great motivator to keep going.

- **Manage your expectations of others.** Be mindful of what you expect from others. Everyone is going through their own journey in life and may not be willing or able to provide you with what you need. Respect where they are and focus on the relationship you want to have.

- **Let go of things that aren't aligned with your priorities.** If it isn't going to help you get to where you want to go, then why are you holding on to it? Explore situations where you might resort to old behaviors and put things on your plate that you don't want. What do you need to let go of that is not aligned with where you want to go?

While there have been very few instances, I have worked with a couple of coaching clients who weren't yet committed to making the change they claimed they wanted for themselves. Some of you will come up with excuses as to why you aren't doing the work: lack of time, resources, etc. If that is the case, then I encourage you to try… and try again. Leverage your grit and give yourself grace because only *you* can do the work.

If you completed the exercises in earlier chapters, you identified more of who you are and what you want. Now, it's time to reset your priorities and take action so you can move toward your vision.

It might help to go back and review your responses to the exercises in the previous chapters, then, review the questions below.

Reflect on the vision you created for yourself. Based on who you want to become and what you want to do, what will it take to move forward? List three to five priorities that will help you move toward your vision.

_____

_____

_____

_____

_____

_____

_____

_____

_____

_____

_____

_____

_____

_____

_____

_____

_____

_____

_____

What needs to come off your plate? What do you need to let go of to move toward your vision? Consider things that aren't in alignment with who you want to be, what you want to do, and where you are exerting unnecessary energy.

What actions will help you move toward your vision? List three to
five actions you can take based on the priorities you identified.

Who can help you achieve your vision? Consider who can help you in achieving your priorities and carrying out the actions you want to take. Reflect on the specific request you need to make and be prepared to explain why it is important to you. Consider explaining the benefit for them as well if it requires their buy-in.

KEY TAKEAWAYS

Principle #3: It's never too late to rediscover what is important to *you*.

1. Commit to a new path and adjust actions to align with what is important—to *you*.

2. Identify the behaviors and habits that are no longer serving you well.

3. Be willing to take risks and get uncomfortable.

4. Conflict is inevitable, so have the hard conversations

5. There is no time limit on when to start, but you may not be here tomorrow. Why wait?

PRINCIPLE #4

Amid adversity, you can reclaim power through choice.

CHAPTER 10

Yours for the Taking

"Strength doesn't come from the things you can do. It comes from overcoming the things you once thought you couldn't."
— Rikki Rogers

There were many challenges I had to overcome in my life—navigating my divorce amicably, an unexpected pregnancy, moving across the country on my own, and then the passing of my mother, to name a few. In hindsight, I'm amazed at all of the things I have been through and have not only survived but have come out stronger on the other side. There was one challenge I did not anticipate though, one that resurfaces now and then when I feel stuck. That is, the stories I tell myself. At times, that inner voice would say:

"…you won't be able to find a good job…"

"…you can't afford to raise two kids on your own…"

"…you shouldn't uproot your daughter to move across the country…"

"…you won't find a partner who will accept you…"

"…you will never have time to do all of the things you wanted…"

In the midst of adversity, we often lower our expectations of ourselves, and others—or worse, give up altogether. Fear is the most common thing that holds people back from achieving what they want. But fear of what? Have you ever sat down to think about what is *really* holding you back from elevating yourself? When you reflect on something you have always wanted to do, but then find *some* reason to push it aside. Why?

Maybe you don't believe in your ability to achieve that thing you have been wanting to try or don't think you have the resources to accomplish it. Or, possibly, you place blame on other people whom you believe are preventing you from achieving what you want.

I hate to break it to you, but *you* might be part of what is getting in your way. I say that with the utmost compassion in my heart. The question is, what are you going to do about it? I have one suggestion…start by naming it. Name what is getting in your way. You may find that it is your thoughts that are standing between where you are today and where you want to be.

After I moved to Ohio and had my son, I started exploring new jobs. After all, I was unable to stay at home and raise him and my daughter without some sort of income. The thought of finding day-care for Parker at such a young age was scary. I had heard of so many moms who had issues and struggled with that, for various reasons: guilt, not feeling anyone would take care of their child(ren) the way that they would, not to mention the cost of childcare.

I was extremely fortunate to find a job as Director of Human Resources with a startup technology firm, where I stayed for a couple of years. I enjoyed the work I did and the excitement of working at a startup, but it went through some organizational changes and eventually merged with an organization headquartered in Los Angeles, California. Initially, I considered staying on as these kinds of changes bring excitement and plenty of challenges to an organization—which I always found invigorating. But I wasn't up for the challenge this time.

By this time in my life, my mom had passed away. The cancer, which was initially diagnosed as lung cancer, had spread to her bones and lymph nodes. It was my first time losing one of the most important people in my life—the only person who understood me and what I was going through as a single parent. I was also enrolled in the Executive Coaching program at Case Western Reserve University, which I thought would help elevate my skills and give me a new focus—something positive to look forward to; something to challenge my thinking and refocus my energy. For many years prior, I knew I was ready to make a change, but never took the time to think about what it was I wanted to do next in my career. Then, I came across a role with a small consulting firm that would position me well for where I am today.

I ended up leaving the technology company and going to the firm as an Organizational Development Consultant. I had always dreamed of going into consulting, but for those who may not know, consultants are known to travel up to 80% or more of the time. Obviously, having full-time responsibility for raising two kids, that much travel was not going to fit into my lifestyle. But this role was primarily in the Cleveland area, so it allowed me to dip my toes in that world and try it on for size, so to speak. That was one of the best moves I could have made, as it catapulted me to where I am now, managing my own business.

I worked there for close to four years and was fortunate to have wonderful opportunities to work with clients, develop new skills, and stretch myself. I learned a lot about myself in that time and had to adapt to fit within the culture—more so than at any other organization I have worked for. While that was very difficult, I looked back and realized it was also helpful. I learned a lot about my own behavior, what motivates me, and how to better adapt to change. More importantly, I realized that I didn't want to compromise on what is most important to me. No job, paycheck, or material possessions will be worth my or my family's well-being and happiness.

It was spring, and I was still processing my mom's death when my dad started having health complications, requiring me to travel back and forth to New York, as he lived alone and needed help.

Parker was also having challenges at school. I would later learn that he was a kid who had different needs, and the schools in which I had him enrolled weren't equipped to support his needs in a way that would help him flourish. There were a few instances when the school would call to inform me of an incident Parker was involved in—and had, at times, started. One day in particular, I can recall the school calling to tell me about some challenges they were having with him…again. It wasn't working out. The school wasn't equipped to work with his development needs, and they'd had enough.

It turns out that in addition to having Attention Deficit Hyperactivity Disorder (ADHD), it seemed Parker had sensory issues, which caused him to be sensitive to sounds, lights, and textures. He was an extremely curious kid, so it was hard to prevent him from doing things, and he moved fast, so he got into a lot of things! I would cut the tags from his clothes to prevent him from having daily meltdowns; his socks had to be put on exactly right so the seams lined up with his toes, and his pants couldn't have pockets in the back that would rub on the inside. He fully explored his environment, often putting things in his mouth. He was one picky eater—as many kids are. There are only certain foods he will eat because of how they feel when he chews them. Unfortunately, I believe his sensory issues also caused him to bite a lot of things, including his friends at school.

So, there I was again: at a fork in the road. Feeling the need to make another tough decision to establish a sense of equilibrium. In a job I loved, but knowing the culture wasn't the right fit for me. I could not be myself, and any remaining energy I had was not worth continuing the façade. I didn't have the flexibility to work from home and was under constant stress. My son's challenges in school were causing me to worry it would eventually impact the work I did with clients, and ultimately hurt my credibility with my boss. My dad was also struggling and regularly needed help back in New York.

So, I decided to leave. And I quit without having another job. That, my friends, is not something I would typically recommend to anyone. Yet, it is a good example of how I operate. I agree to a challenge and figure it out along the way.

I knew I would be okay financially for about six months and still have money in savings, plus I was teaching virtual classes at the University of California, Irvine, so I would have some income coming in. I was excited about the ability to have the summer off, spend time with my kids, go to NY as much as I needed, and just *be*. I started exploring other roles, and was interviewing, but kept telling myself I wasn't going to settle on any job. I had some non-negotiables that would create a line in the sand, so I expected the search to be challenging.

And it was.

Over the next few months, I interviewed with various companies, but nothing caught my attention the way I had hoped. The market was good, so there were plenty of opportunities, but I had a vision of being in a strategic role, having creative control, leading, and having the flexibility I so desperately needed. I wanted freedom not only at work but to integrate work *and* life in a way that was best for me.

I continued teaching and started getting called on by people who heard I had left the consulting firm. Now, I was picking up projects without having to do much business development. Those projects continued coming in, and later that fall, I took a leap of faith and created an LLC to make it official. I called my business Talent Principles. My focus would be "Connecting talent and purpose to drive performance". My mission would be to help individuals, teams, and organizations ensure that people were in the right roles, aligned with the collective purpose of the team, and clear on the mission of the organization. I dove headfirst into my work. As of today, I have been in business for almost five years and have grown year over year. I'm leveraging my strengths, doing work I love—the way I want to— and can prioritize my time to be with my family.

Truthfully, those "stories" continue to flood my mind now and then:

"…you will fail if you start your own business…"

"…you are failing as a mom…"

"…you should listen to people with more experience…"

Thankfully, I now have increased awareness of when that inner voice takes over and ruminates on all of the negative, fixed-thinking. When I find myself stuck for too long, I choose to reclaim what I want and carve out my own path. It is usually not an easy path, but I am grateful every time I take the risk.

In the past, my ex-husband would tell me I should go into consulting. While I had always been curious about it, he saw something in me that I hadn't seen quite yet. Ironically, he was in consulting too, and being married to him (while he traveled about 80% of the time) didn't allow me to achieve the same dream. Or at least, I didn't even try to consider it back then. His job seemed to put me at a lifelong disadvantage, with what seemed like little choice at the time.

While I don't have any regrets, I can't help but wonder if I would have made the same decisions then, knowing what I know now. If we, as a couple, would have made the same decisions. I suspect we probably would. It seems that one of the logical responses to who should stay home with the kids is the one who makes less money in their job. Additionally, society places the expectation on the mom to stay home—as if it were set on some type of default. My income couldn't compare with what my ex-husband made. I was tired of competing.

My identity is not defined by how much money I make, and I will be damned if I will let my role as a single mom define me too.

While I want to be paid my worth—and believe I add a lot of value to my clients—money is not a driver for me. I measure my success by business growth, of course, and saving for the future, but I stay focused on what is in front of me. I try not to ruminate too long on the past anymore—unless it is to reflect and learn. Now, I think about the next step I need to take that will move me closer to my vision. Then, I aim and act.

The other measures of success for me are based on quality time with not just my kids, but with my sister and her family, my dad, and my close friends. I want to prioritize my time to do creative things, like writing more books and creating new programs for my clients. Plus, I want to live abroad someday. Could I have those things working in Corporate America? Maybe. But I know for sure I wouldn't have the level of autonomy, drive, and ability to innovate that I do now, running my own business. I am right where I am meant to be and when I get off track again, I will reclaim what is mine...again, and again.

My Most Important Assignment

I have been a mom for seventeen years now, and I suppose if I were applying for a job as a mom somewhere, one might say I'm an expert. Let me be the first one to say I'm not. Despite all the books on parenting, there is no crucial rule book or tutorial outlining the experiences and feelings moms have throughout the many years of raising children to become exactly who they are meant to be—at least, none that I have ever found.

If anyone had told me when I was younger and dreaming of getting married and having kids just how hard this job was with all the sacrifices and hard work that would come along with it, I am not sure that I would have signed up for it. Honestly. Being a mom is an all-day, every day, 24/7 job. I certainly would have been more thoughtful and asked more questions in that "interview"!

If I had known of the lack of appreciation I would experience at times from my kids (and ex-husband when I was married), the rollercoaster of emotions I would have to endure, or that I would end up parenting on my own, I might have run away from it all...as fast and far as I could. Hands down, being a single parent with the responsibilities I have had over the years is the most difficult thing I have ever done on my own...okay, writing this book is close in comparison!

Yet, I am so glad I was "none the wiser", as they say. I can tell you now that I do not regret one moment of my life—including having kids, despite all the challenges of being a mom. You see, all those experiences have made me who I am today, and there is no doubt that my kids have made me a better person—a better coach at work and a more patient mom at home. For that, I hope they know how grateful I am for what they have taught me.

A key leadership capability that I help clients develop has been instrumental in helping me grow as a parent, and that is strengthening my emotional intelligence (EQ). For those of you who may not be familiar with EQ, there are four primary elements, which are described as [7]:

1. **Self-Awareness**: Knowing who *you* are—your strengths, weaknesses, and biases. For example, understanding your personality style and how you communicate allows you to gain insight into tendencies you are likely to demonstrate when interacting with others.

2. **Self-Regulation**: The ability to utilize the information you know about yourself to effectively regulate your emotions (leveraging strengths and keeping unproductive tenden-

cies in check). If you have an expressive personality, like to share ideas, and tend to talk a lot, you may need to focus on active listening to allow others to feel heard and acknowledged.

3. **Social Awareness**: Knowing and understanding *others* and the ability to read social cues and understand group dynamics. An example of this would be understanding the personality styles or communication preferences of those around you. So, if your partner is more of an introvert and doesn't express their emotions openly, it provides insight into their needs and how to best approach them to have more productive and constructive conversations.

4. **Relationship Management**: Leveraging what you know about yourself *and* others to manage interactions to create positive outcomes, which may be achieved through collaborating with others, or effectively managing conflict with someone. Given the example above—you have an expressive style while your partner has more of an introverted style—how you manage those differences is important. To improve communication, you may need to compose your emotions and communicate your thoughts objectively and logically, so your partner receives the information better. It's about adapting to the needs of others based on your knowledge, demonstrating empathy, and working together to solve issues and improve relationships.

As you can probably imagine, these skills are essential as a parent. One day while on a call with a client, he made a comment that struck me. Honestly, I thought I would never hear this from anyone, especially during what turned out to be a tumultuous day for me in the middle of the COVID-19 pandemic.

"You manage your emotions well and always seem controlled," he said. I was laughing on the inside because he didn't have a front-row view of the shit-show that sometimes takes place in my home. Many days I didn't feel like I had it all together, and I would soon be put to the test in front of my client.

As many parents were experiencing at the time, I had the "luxury" of being home with my kids while I also tried to conduct video calls with clients…all while maintaining my composure. As you can imagine, I was not always good at this, especially given my personality style, and that of my son.

Kids are active at all growing stages as they learn boundaries, manners, and how to control their emotions. My son has all the typical urges and challenges of being a child, in addition to managing the unique and sometimes isolating behaviors of ADHD, and a new diagnosis of anxiety. At times, he has difficulty managing impulses (characteristics can vary from person to person). His anxiety also causes his emotions to escalate very quickly, which to others can seem like an unreasonable overreaction at times.

While on the call with my client, my son came into my office because he wanted to watch TV (he was bored being on his virtual classroom call). When I said, "No," he reacted by screaming back at me and trying to throw papers on the floor. I could feel my heart rate increasing and my patience starting to wane. Worse, thoughts of how my client must be thinking to himself, "Control your kid," were going through my head—negative stories that left me feeling like a "bad mom".

This created a very stressful situation as I was sitting in front of my client, trying to compose myself and not react to what was happening right next to me.

This is exactly where self-management skills are essential. I had to take charge and put on my armor, or I surely would have crumbled at that moment—revealing how little control I had and was feeling on the inside. As I felt my heart pounding out of my chest, I could feel my body temperature start to rise. It was like watching the red line on a thermometer quickly rise after being placed in a pot of boiling water. That is what I felt like and I was trying my hardest to not boil over in front of my client.

I took a deep breath and reminded myself that I was being watched. Not just by my client, but also by my son. How I react in tough situations is how I teach him to react—yet another daily practice for me. Thankfully, my client was understanding. It helped that I was able to hit "mute" before things escalated.

Looking back now, I know I had more power than I gave myself credit for, but sometimes it is hard to admit when we can achieve and overcome difficult things. Occasionally, we focus on what went wrong and ruminate on "fixing" the situations, or even thinking we can fix people. Reflecting on these moments, I realize we don't need "fixing"; we must reclaim what we want, give ourselves grace, learn, and move on.

The impact parenting a neurodivergent child has had on me (and our household) can be swift, be out of the blue, and deflate any sense of confidence I have as a mom. Worse, some interactions I have with my son are often followed by his gut-wrenching words, *"You are the meanest mom ever!"* I constantly have to remind myself that he struggles to find effective ways to communicate his feelings, so rather than internalize his words, I try to help him find ways to express what he is feeling and needs from me.

Suffice it to say that my emotional capacity to manage intense situations continues to grow effectively, but it is a continuous work in progress. I don't always respond well, and on some days, I find myself starting to believe those gut-wrenching words myself. But thanks to the work I do, and have done on myself, I have developed an awareness of my tendencies and know what I need to do to improve the relationship I have with my son...and the kind of relationship I have with myself. So, I work on reacting differently by taking a breath, walking away, and letting things go now and then. Every. Single. Day.

I gauge my success by asking myself if I am satisfied with how I respond to these situations. If the answer is yes, I will move on. If the answer is no, I reflect and consider how I will handle it better next go-round…as there is more certainly going to be another opportunity around the corner.

It, therefore, made me laugh inside when my client said that I appeared to "be in control", as I don't always have it together! At the end of the day, if I have learned new things to support my development and developed stronger, more trusting relationships with my children, then I say that is a success. I remind myself that no one ever has all the answers or is spot on with anything ALL of the time, so I look at my successes and remind myself when I do mess up, that I am human. And, if I hurt someone in the process, I do my best and take steps to do the right thing and apologize to rebuild trust with them.

The bottom line is that when things get tough, that is your biggest opportunity to practice the very skills you are trying to develop. So, despite the shit-show that was going on in my household, I was able to flex some muscles I don't use often, to develop new behaviors—behaviors that are more aligned with who I want to be, and that support the relationship I want with those around me.

RECLAIMING WHAT YOU WANT

I recently came across an exercise I did within a leadership development program I developed for a client a few years ago. It was an exercise that helped people identify what was preventing them from creating the change they wanted in their lives. I completed the worksheet and identified a commitment I wanted to make to myself that would propel me forward. That commitment read, "To take risks and trust myself more…". At the end of that worksheet was a box that was titled "Success", where I asked people to describe how they would measure success after achieving their commitment to themselves. In that box I wrote, "I've written a book and will make changes I believe are necessary to have a positive impact on others." I also wrote, "I am confident and committed to the actions I take based on what *I* want." Finding that worksheet as I write this book and sharing it with all of you couldn't be a better testament to reclaiming what you want.

So, my dear friends, what do you want to reclaim?

During times when you feel stuck and unable to move toward your vision, step back and gain perspective. You may realize that you are uncomfortable simply because you are asking yourself—and sometimes others—to do something different. If you can remind yourself where you are headed and that this temporary discomfort is just that—temporary—you can gain confidence to take one more step forward. Then, know that the discomfort others are feeling is also temporary, so they will eventually get over it. If they don't, it isn't your problem to fix.

Many of the leadership capabilities I coach others to develop transfer to the role of a parent. This is especially the case when it comes to developing emotional intelligence. You have to know yourself and understand what behaviors and actions are getting in your way of achieving what you want. Just as important, you have to consider those around you who may be impacted by your journey. Then, work together to ensure there is alignment on what you need to move toward your goals. The hard part is doing the work and holding yourself—and others—accountable. And getting right back on your feet when things go sideways.

Sometimes we fail to identify the right issue we are trying to solve, and instead, react to what we *think* is the issue. An easy example is when I get upset because one of the kids spilled the milk. While that might be frustrating, it's really not about the milk. It's about the fact that I'm always the one cleaning it up. The real issue is I'm angry. I am the one having to do everything and I'm scared that it will always be the case. That makes me feel alone. *That* is the real issue.

The hard work you will have to do is digging deep down into those feelings you have to figure out what the real barrier is. Only when you understand what your true obstacle is, can you gain clarity on how to overcome it.

In the next chapter, I'm going to give you a head start and share some of the potential barriers that could be getting in your way. As you review them, see if any resonate with you. If they don't, explore for yourself what could be holding you back from creating the change you crave.

Don't give up because you feel stuck. Take the next step and move into your personal freedom.

Endnotes

(7)   Travis Bradberry, Emotional Intelligence 2.0: Hardcover (Barnes & Noble, June 16, 2009).

CHAPTER 11

Name It to Tame It

"You must do the thing you think you cannot do."
– Eleanor Roosevelt

I'm sure you can attest, there is no greater teacher in life than our children. They can be brutally honest without blinking an eye, which can sometimes cut through your heart like a dagger. They can notice and sense things that elude adults because they are not looking through a skewed lens. I have found that my most significant and most challenging situations to practice my leadership skills are at home with my kids and even with friends and family.

Some days I feel confident about my role as a mom. Other days, I feel myself pulled into thoughts of negativity and even loneliness in a full, and at times, chaotic house. I have felt that "no one understands" or "no one else is dealing with this!" Yes, I have my days sitting in the self-loathing, fixed mindset, for a little too long. But then I step back and gain perspective, "get over it and move on," as my son would say. In the summer camp he attended one year through the Cleveland Clinic, which supports kids who are neurodivergent, he learned the phrase, "G.O.M.O", which stands for "get over it and move on". I understand that I cannot stay down even if I want to, not only because it leaves space for me to have a pity party for myself—

which I know is unhealthy—but more importantly because my kids are watching. That is not how I will teach them the importance of resiliency.

There are common barriers that prevent people, particularly women, and especially moms, from living life to its fullest—even with the best plan in place. The key is to stay focused on nourishing and supporting efforts to live out the best life you can, instead of adding things that will be toxic and spread disease. In this chapter, we will explore the common barriers I see women (myself included) struggle with, that keep us from achieving our potential. As you review these barriers, make notes next to the ones that resonate with you and anything else that brings to the surface potential obstacles that may get in your way of achieving the vision you established for yourself.

Are you ready to dig deep?

BARRIER #1: GUILT

So, what gets in your way of caring for yourself and doing the things you want for yourself? If I had to guess the most common reason moms say, it is one word: GUILT. This often stems from behavior that conflicts with what your conscience says. In certain instances, you may do something but feel like you should have done something different, causing you to feel the urge to remedy the situation, like apologize or give in to someone's request...even when you don't want to. Don't get me wrong, sometimes guilt serves a legitimate purpose—maybe to teach us a lesson.[8]

At other times, guilt does not serve us so well. Many of you have likely experienced, at one time or another, a feeling of guilt over doing things that you believe you maybe *should* be doing for others but aren't (or can't). Or it may be a belief that you shouldn't feel a certain way when you genuinely *do* feel that way! The degree to which people feel guilt varies.

Guilt is a feeling of responsibility or remorse for an offense—real or imagined. It can create self-imposed pressure to own someone else's feelings even when you have not done anything wrong. The pressure may come from beliefs you hold to be true in your mind, whether they are true or not. Guilt can come from anywhere and stays with you wherever you go...especially for moms. Am I doing enough for my kids? Did I do something to upset others? Should I volunteer more at school or work? Should I help more with homework? Should I cancel a night out with friends or that planned trip? "I should have...", No wonder we all feel overwhelmed—guilt can surface daily in the most basic ways.

An example of how this plays out in my house is when my son asks me to get him a glass of milk, and I say, "Nope. You are capable of getting your own glass of milk," and he responds with, "You are the meanest mom ever!" I sometimes have to catch myself or those feelings start welling up inside my heart...feelings of guilt. Maybe I *should* get him his milk. Wouldn't a "good mom" do that for her child? The feelings are not a result of doing anything wrong, per se; they are from hearing his response in the abrasive and accusatory tone of displeasure with me—one that I have probably heard in the past as a child. Then, I'm not just feeling guilty, I'm also comparing myself: a two-for-one, if you will.

Guilt can also be something placed on other people to get them to do something. I suspect many moms have done this over the years—with good intentions! I know I certainly have. Whether it was my unreasonable reaction, or the tone in my voice saying, "It's okay. I'm fine if you want to spend Christmas at your dad's this year." Guilt can coerce people to do things that they really don't want to do but may give in simply because they don't want to deal with the potential ramifications. Assess how guilt shows up for you and in the next chapter we will look at suggested remedies.

It is possible that you may feel guilty for taking time for yourself, and the response from others may magnify those feelings. You deserve, and likely desperately *need*, that time. It is important to recognize that when you constantly give to others and don't prioritize yourself, you potentially send the message that you don't matter as much or are not as important as others. Alternatively, it may teach others not to prioritize their own needs—further perpetuating the vicious cycle.

My son's approach may cause me on my weaker days to question if I am a mean mom, as he so easily asserts. He is just learning how to get the things he wants in life and needs a few lessons, but the experience is very taxing on me. This is when I explain to him my role in his life is to help him become independent, so doing things he can do on his own is creating a dependency on me.

Someday, he will understand. It may take twenty years, but one day he will look back and realize I taught him to be self-reliant and develop independence. Or maybe not—the point is that I should not feel guilty for trying to establish some independence in my son.

Guilt can motivate us to take steps in the right direction, like apologizing for something we did to offend someone. But when it is something being self-imposed all too often, it will become important to communicate openly with others to set boundaries and respect your decisions, as well as encourage people to express their needs clearly to possibly prevent going down that guilt trip road.

> *"There is no way to be a perfect mother, but*
> *a million ways to be a good one."*
> *– Unknown*

BARRIER #2—COMPARISON

Over the years, I have had people tell me that I appear to have it all together. Many have said they don't know "how I do all that I do" as a single parent and business owner, managing all that life has thrown at me. While I can take that as a compliment, in the sense that at least others don't see the shit-show that goes on in my house at any given time or the self-doubt I experience, it is also a reminder for everyone that things aren't always as they seem. My life didn't fit the proverbial mold of Cinderella. The order of my life didn't play out quite how I had planned or hoped for. I, therefore, compared myself to others. That created a lifelong dance with comparison.

We judge others by what we see on the surface unless we take time to get to know people. When interactions or relationships lack trust and vulnerability, we run the risk of conducting superficial exchanges that are void of depth or any true meaning. Ultimately, when we fail to really connect with people, we never really know who they are—worse, we never share the most intimate, authentic parts of who we are, often out of fear of being judged for who we *really* are.

Everyone has internal demons they are fighting, whether it is in the form of people, hardships, or those horrible thoughts in your head, which sometimes lie to you because they are based on ideas other—often insecure—people put in your head.

I encourage you to remember that when you see a mom who seems to have it all—good looks, a handsome husband or good-looking partner, a nice car, a great job, and a big house—she has challenges *and* a story too. Moreover, she is likely doing her very best to keep others from seeing the pain and insecurities she feels, masking it all to hide her real truth.

When we compare ourselves to others, we lose sight of our identity and uniqueness. We also never win because there is ALWAYS, and I mean ALWAYS, someone better looking, more successful, and smarter; someone who potentially has something you want. Comparison is another form of judgment—which is not productive.

We all have our differences. Comparison, in and of itself, can be helpful to us—in moderation. But if you don't have the self-awareness and ability to manage your reactions, comparison can cause envy of what other people have and keep you locked in a state of constantly looking outward for something to fill a void on the inside. Remember, as I have shared earlier, we also look at people and their lives through a different lens. Things are never as we perceive them to be from the outside looking in.

You may expect that if you get *one* more thing or do this *one* thing, you will be happier. *Things* don't bring us security and happiness—at least not in the long run. As we gain in life, more responsibility typically comes with it. With more responsibility, we have more to concern ourselves with, which depletes time to focus on what is truly important.

Our wealth, material things, and even people can all be taken away in the blink of an eye.

While I still fall prey to comparing myself to others at times, when I catch myself, I acknowledge what they have and recognize that it is what is important to *them*. If it is something I admire and think may fit into what I want for myself, I explore that further before thinking it will make me happier, prettier, more successful, etc. Conversely, if you tend to look at others and judge them because they appear worse off than you, it is still a form of comparison.

After all, when you judge others, what does it say about *you*? Is that the person you are trying to become or want to be known as?

"Good Mom" Syndrome

When my son doesn't get what he wants or when I do something that doesn't align with his goals, he often calls me the "meanest mom". Though I know this is circumstantial and will pass, that he doesn't mean it, let me tell you, there are many days I believe his hurtful words.

Would a "good mom" request that others get what they want from the kitchen rather than waiting on them with every request? Would a "good mom" say "no" to their kids who want to do something fun, and instead take a nap to get some much-needed rest?

Or would a "good mom" yell at her kids because they dropped their food on the kitchen floor again? If you can relate to this, you probably would agree that it isn't about food on the floor; it's about all the things that have preceded that incident that you are still feeling resentful for and haven't properly addressed.

It is about the fact that you are the one who generally must clean up after others, and it is usually after the tenth request not to play at the table, knowing that the food would eventually end up all over the floor. And, knowing it will likely happen again.

One of the biggest barriers you can face as a mom is the limiting beliefs you have regarding what a "good mom" is. That definition has been generally defined as:

- being all consumed with your kids,
- always being nice to others,
- never saying no,
- maintaining a spotless home,
- being in perfect shape,
- for some, maybe holding down a career, and
- …having a "perfect" life (at least as observed from the outside).

In the process of trying to live out this unrealistic expectation, or one not meant for all of us, we question ourselves. We wonder if we are meeting the expectations of others rather than our own expectations of the type of mom we want to be for our own family. These generalized expectations are harmful to everyone involved.

"Comparison is the thief of joy."
– Theodore Roosevelt

BARRIER #3: RESENTMENT (A.K.A. FEELING MOMGRY)

I suspect that one of the biggest barriers that holds moms back from achieving what they want is underlying resentment. Yet, you may not even realize this deeply hidden feeling is the key to unlocking your very own freedom. I believe that a mom's resentment stems from deep, deep, I mean *deep*, frustrations of doing everything for everyone, all the time. It is the proverbial "role" people believe moms have, and that is to take care of everyone, everywhere, all the time. Feeling "momgry" is what happens when a mom gets angry about the responsibilities that are perceived to be hers and only hers. Sometimes, those responsibilities are self-imposed.

Resentment can take on the form of bitterness toward someone for feeling treated unfairly, feeling betrayed, or not feeling supported. Sadly, sometimes it is hard to even recognize it when you feel it— whether that is from denial or not thinking it is acceptable—so you don't admit it to yourself. Worse, you may resent yourself.

Maybe it takes on the form of people taking advantage of you at home, assuming that you will make dinner, do the laundry, make lunches, or take time off to get the kids to their appointments. Or it could be the fact that every time a mess is made, the family leaves it because it is seen as Mom's job to clean it up. Or maybe, just maybe, it is because you have conditioned others to believe it is your job, primarily because you keep volunteering for the role. Here is a great meme I saw recently that sums up this idea. It reads:

Me: I need some help around here.
Also Me: No, not like that. Here, I'll do it.

You get the picture, right? How many of you take on responsibilities because you like things done a certain way or you don't believe others are doing it as well as you could? Like when your partner doesn't fold the laundry right, or when your daughter didn't load the dishwasher as efficiently as you could (Yep. I was guilty of that!). This can also happen at work and throughout your career.

The point is, if you are feeling frustrated as a mom, consider what is contributing to the frustration and how much of that is self-imposed. You might have to take a hard look in the mirror and do some explaining…to yourself, that is.

Even if the feelings of resentment that you are experiencing aren't due to something you caused yourself, you must still identify what is contributing to your feelings and work through them. Those feelings could be coming from beliefs you are carrying about your role as a mom, or that you don't have clear boundaries set for yourself.

Feeling resentful will hold you back because it keeps you in fight-or-flight mode when you are stressed, which perpetuates a fixed mindset and can leave you feeling like a victim. That, in turn, can cause you to place blame on others, preventing you from moving forward because you are constantly looking in the rearview mirror. Your future is waiting for you to show up. What are you waiting for?

"Resentment is like drinking poison and
waiting for the other person to die."
– Carrie Fisher

BARRIER #4—THE NEED FOR CONTROL

As a single mom, I sometimes feel maintaining control is the only thing that keeps my family going. One little detail out of place can derail any perfectly oiled engine. This can take on many different forms, from taking on everything yourself to ensure things are done just the way you want, to trying to control what other people do, say, or even think of you. Don't think that is possible? Trust me. I have tried many times over the years! As moms, we often have more to do than humanly possible, so we get in "mission" mode. This mode can spill over into other areas of our lives, including relationships, if we aren't careful. And I hate to break it to you, but never ever will you be able to control anyone else.

There is plenty of research out there that suggests that having a sense of control can improve your health. It helps us to have agency over ourselves to achieve our goals in life. But you know what they say…too much of a good thing isn't *always* good. Besides, are the things you are trying to control really yours to own, or for someone else to act on?

Feeling the need for control over things, people, and circumstances all the time can have negative consequences. Think of any experience you may have had working for a boss who micromanages people, nitpicking everything or telling you how to accomplish every step of a task. Or maybe it is having to be involved in everything to ensure it is done exactly the way you want it. This can be exhausting for everyone. It provides no room for people to breathe, and it stunts growth. Being overly controlling prevents children from developing their own agency and erodes trust. Providing children with the opportunity to discover who they are and to believe they are competent and capable is crucial to cultivating a greater sense of self. Self-esteem comes from the daily experiences that provide opportunities to explore who we are.[9] The same applies to your relationships with your partner or spouse. I have yet to meet anyone who likes to be controlled by someone else.

When you consider the amount of mental space and energy the brain requires when focused on too many things, you can imagine the result. I don't know about you, but my ability to remember every little detail required to maintain a household, run a business, and raise two kids runs thin many days. That is the very reason I need to be selective about what things I decide to control, and identify things that aren't that important, or don't require my oversight.

Another perspective to consider is the energy you may put into trying to control what the future holds. As you think about your decisions and how you operate, do you at times manipulate situations so that they align with more of what you envisioned for yourself? Do you find it hard to just let life take its course some days?

Some people are more wired to control situations, and even people, while others are fine with letting others take over. Some people just feel more secure and confident when they have control over things, whether that is over a situation, over people, or even over their emotions. Control is only an illusion, and striving for more can bring increased stress and conflict. Are there areas of your life that you are trying to control that may be holding you back?

"You can't control everything. Sometimes you just need
to relax and have faith that things will work out."
– Kody Keplinger

BARRIER #5—EXCESSIVE DEFERENCE

When people are overly willing to serve others and place more regard on another's wishes, they may be showing excessive deference. You have likely learned something from your parents or the parental figures you had growing up, and at times, may yield to the opinions of others as if you were still that child looking for direction from someone wiser. People defer to others for various reasons. Some defer too much to a boss or colleague and fail to take hold of their career and find their footing. Some people do it in their marriage, and some defer to their parents for various reasons.

Having the tendency to defer to others too much, whether that is your partner, a boss, your friends, or even your child(ren) can prevent you from flexing that decision-making muscle, causing it to atrophy. When muscles atrophy, they become weak. When your muscles are weak, you will be unable to move confidently with conviction. Showing deference to others may be intended to show respect or be accepted, or it could be done as a way to avoid conflict with others. Yet when done excessively, it can become a barrier that is deeply woven into actions, or even inactions, that prevent you from moving forward on your own path. Instead, you end up living your life according to what others want—or believe—is best for you.

When you excessively defer to others on things, you not only disempower yourself, but you can also give others the perception that you lack confidence in your decision-making. This can result in people not trusting in your decision-making abilities and can potentially erode their respect for you.

This does not suggest you shouldn't honor and respect your parents, your partner, or other important people in your life. Rather, it is essential to show respect for others and yourself—and understand where decision-making authority lies. Context is important. If you need to make a decision regarding something that impacts your family, then you will likely need to discuss and align with those people who are immediately impacted. However, in cases relating to your own well-being and goals, how often are you deferring to others for input or guidance on your decisions? You can address issues that need to be addressed and do so respectfully. Whether at work, at home, or in social settings with friends, empower yourself and speak candidly about issues you believe to be important.

People will give you feedback based on what *they* think is best based on their own experiences and likely what they also know about you. Now, some might say that is a good thing—gaining perspectives from others can be helpful, opening our eyes to new and different ways that we might not have considered. However, if you tend to make decisions based on whether others will like you or make decisions so that others don't get upset with you, then you will constantly be living out the dreams of others, rather than your own.

Achieving what you want in life requires influencing others, and sometimes making tough decisions. If you are constantly deferring to what others think as it relates to the goals you have, I would encourage you to ask yourself why and to explore what it is you truly fear.

"If you live for people's acceptance, you will die from their rejection."
– *Lecrae Moore*

BARRIER #6—TIME CONSTRAINTS

We all have the same amount of time, and even though we know just how much of this resource we get each day, this is one barrier that I find people struggling with. At times, even I still do.

Many things contribute to your ability to "manage time". Though you can't change the fact that there are only twenty-four hours in any given day, you likely do your best to cram as much as you can into every one of them. If you operate like me some days, maybe you are also trying to cram 730 days of work into 365 days each year. How's that working for you?

Typically, what I see is that people are overwhelmed with competing priorities—they are double-booking themselves, saying yes to things that aren't important or urgent, and losing sight of what is important. These competing priorities are coupled with the need to improve their time management skills, which is critical for any human being to master—regardless of how old they are. I want to add that being overwhelmed by these conflicts is not intentional; rather, I believe people succumb to their circumstances or environment, and even to their approach to getting things done.

It is a common challenge moms experience, particularly moms who also work outside the home, which comes with additional complexities and managing the vast responsibilities across work and home life. Other things contribute to not managing time effectively, like not having good systems in place to track responsibilities; another possibility is that your approach to working through your priorities could be inefficient. Or possibly you underestimate how much time it takes to complete tasks.

Given some of the previous barriers shared, you may be experiencing a few all at once. If you tend to take on too much out of the desire to control things, then that will contribute to your ability to manage your time. This is why it is so important to explore what is important—your actions and behaviors—and get to the core of why you do what you do.

I don't foresee a day when someone is going to be that innovative and find a way to cram more hours into the day. After all, don't you want relief from the need to control everything? Don't you want more time in your day to focus on what is most important to you? Furthermore, don't you want to spend your time on things that align with your values and what will help you achieve your future potential? Or are you spending time on things that are based on what other people value, or beliefs that don't reflect who you are?

"The lost time is never found again."
– Benjamin Franklin

Endnotes

(8) "Guilt," Psychology Today, March 22, 2022, https://www.psychologytoday.com/us/basics/guilt.

  • Holly Brians Ragusa, "Guilt Trip: Is This Emotion Driving Your Life?" Psychology Today, March 22, 2022, https://www.psychologytoday.com/us/blog/duty-to-self/202401/guilt-trip-is-this-emotion-driving-your-life.

(9) A. Maslow, "A Theory of Human Motivation," Psychological Review 50 (1943): 370-396.

CHAPTER 12

Creating a New Narrative

RECLAIM: WORKBOOK

*"The pen that writes your life story must
be held in your own hand."*
– Irene C. Kassorla

Achieving what you want isn't all that hard. Overcoming the barriers to achieving what you want is often where the discomfort lies. While there are some obstacles you might be able to overcome for good, I would guess the vast majority of them will creep back into your life now and then, so learning how to manage them can increase the odds of achieving what you want for yourself.

Principle #4 is "Amid adversity, you can reclaim power through choice." Now that you have a better sense of what might be getting in your way when things get tough, it is time to put the principle into practice and identify new choices you can make. While this is not an exhaustive list of solutions, it may provide you with some ideas to experiment with to see what works for *you*. The suggestions that follow assume you have taken the initial step to identify what might be getting in your way, which is all about gaining self-awareness. Now, you need to take actions to self-manage to move toward your personal vision.

Managing Barrier #1: Guilt

Check the stories you are telling yourself and reframe your thinking. Reflect on the facts of the situation and check your motives. Were you thoughtful in how you approached the situation? Was there good intent in your actions and what you said? Or did you intend to hurt someone or purposefully manipulate the situation? If your actions were intended to better someone, clarify your intent, and apologize if necessary. You don't need to take ownership of someone else being upset about something you did simply to diffuse the situation. You take ownership when you have done something wrong. Don't get sucked into people's negative responses about situations.

Set boundaries. One step toward setting boundaries is asking yourself if you have control over the situation. If you don't, then it might make it easier to not allow yourself to feel guilt; again, this requires good self-awareness of your thoughts and feelings about situations so you can take appropriate action. You could also start by asking if the situation requires you to fix it, or does that responsibility fall on someone else? If it is not yours to fix, that establishes a clear boundary to set some distance between yourself and guilt.

Other ways you can set boundaries for yourself are related to the time and energy you devote to doing things and even being around people. Consider these examples:

- Explore what drains you emotionally. If there are people, things, or places that suck the life out of you, create limits on the time spent in those areas.
- Choose to spend time on things that align with what is important to you. Recognize when you need to stand your ground when challenged by others because they don't agree.
- When you recognize you are deprived of rest, nutrition, or other basic needs, choose to recharge yourself—and ask for help from others, when needed.

Manage your behavior. At times, you may be the one trying to guilt someone else into doing something. If that is the case, then check your motives. Reflect on those behaviors and ask yourself if they are aligned with the person you want to be, and how you want others to feel when they interact with you. You may be causing others to feel guilty, which can impact your relationship, and it will be important for you to consider how to repair the wrongdoing—real or perceived. Rather than inflicting guilt on others, reflect on how you are feeling about the situation and find a way to communicate how you are feeling and identify what you need to ask for. That will help build trust and could improve the relationship.

Give yourself grace. People make mistakes. We are all human, after all. If you identify situations where you tend to make others feel guilty about something, do the right thing. That might mean changing your behavior in the future to minimize making others feel guilty; it might mean you apologize to people, including yourself.

Guilt can be crippling and does not lead to change. Admitting guilt doesn't cure you of it, either. Deal with it honestly and work through the experience of what has caused it—and the impact it has had on you, and others.

Managing Barrier #2: Comparison

Comparison occurs when you evaluate yourself against someone else—whether based on similarities or dissimilarities. You likely compare yourself to others, and people likely compare themselves to you too. When you look at other people, you establish a perception based on your own biases, beliefs, and feelings about something. Maybe it is how they dress, their hair, what they do, or the things they say. When those things don't align with what you like or believe, you make a judgment about it. It's not right or wrong, but it is a judgment. If you believe you have more things, are prettier, are skinnier, are more accomplished or are more educated, you likely perceive yourself as being "better than". However, if you perceive another person to be "better than" you, you may view yourself as less worthy. Here are some considerations that can help overcome comparing yourself to others.

- **Know your value.** Everyone has distinct talents, skills, characteristics, and physical attributes that make them unique. How you do something is special only to you based on your lived experiences, knowledge, and abilities. Your physical traits embody what has been given to you… identify and acknowledge the beautiful things about who you are and listen to them. Show the world what you, and only you, can uniquely do, and the special qualities that make you who you are.
- **Value others.** Recognize that everyone is unique and when you see something you like or admire, acknowledge it and, if possible, share your thoughts with that person. That helps to elevate them to build their confidence. Show empathy as well, to help others feel seen and heard. You never know what is going on behind closed doors. Lift other people up

when you see them looking good and achieving things—even when it may stir up negative feelings for you. Doing so can make others feel valued and recognized, which in turn, can be rewarding for you. Some days, there is no greater feeling than to be seen by others.

- **Check your assumptions**. When you take time to get to know people and understand them for who they are, you can learn a lot. Our first impression of others is based on judgments we make about how they look, behaviors they demonstrate, etc., and it is often based on a lack of information. When you spend time getting to know and gaining knowledge about people, it allows you to develop a better understanding. As you learn more over time, you can build stronger connections, which allows for respect to develop and differences to be valued.

- **Avoid triggers.** Social media and news are flooded with images, opinions, and noise. Do you compare yourself to the images on social media? Is it at work? Is it with certain people? Identify the situations or triggers that stir up emotions in you that leave you feeling less than, unworthy. Acknowledge situations where you compare yourself to others and then explore steps you can take to stay on your path and develop a stronger belief in yourself and what you have to offer this world.

- **Practice gratitude.** Even in the midst of life's challenges there are things to be grateful for. They are opportunities to learn about who you are and what you care about. Reflecting on and writing down the things that bring you joy and happiness can provide perspective and keep you focused on your priorities. That might be supportive relationships you have, new things you are learning, and the progress you are making toward the things you want to achieve. Expressing gratitude for these things can help shift your focus off of others and back on what is important to you.

Who you are is unique and cannot be claimed if you are trying to emulate someone else.

Decide for yourself that living out your purpose in life is the true reward, which is special to only you. Your success will never look like that of another, and if it does, then you are a copy. Is that what you want? How you differ from others is what makes you unique. Embrace it.

Managing Barrier #3: Resentment (a.k.a. Feeling Momgry)

Reflect on your feelings. Before you can take any action to resolve resentment, you have to explore what might be contributing to the feelings you are having. Going back to some of the exercises in Chapter 3 should provide some perspective if you completed those steps. Feelings are generated by our thoughts. The challenge is that those thoughts can sometimes be based on lies, false beliefs, and stories in our minds. This means that you may be feeling something that isn't based on truth or reality. Once you identify the feelings, pause and test your assumptions. Trace back the thoughts that generated it and confirm they are accurate. This may help you avoid those negative feelings in the future. Ultimately, there may be some form of forgiveness that is needed to move through feelings of resentment. You may need to forgive someone, or maybe even yourself.

Process your feelings. When you bottle up negative feelings for a long time, they have nowhere to go. When they brew long enough over time, you run the risk of those emotions coming out in unproductive ways. Some examples might include physical stress, like headaches, or you may blow up at people around you, which can be triggered by the smallest thing. Additionally, when you don't deal with your feelings, you may begin to disassociate from other feelings you have, potentially making you numb. It is critical to release your negative energy in a safe way that doesn't harm you or others. That might include exercising or talking with people you trust. It can also help to get out into nature and, if needed, scream at the top of your lungs. If you do this, I recommend you go where no one else will hear you! Alternatively, screaming into or punching a pillow could do the trick!

Forgive others. When you hold on to past hurts or things that people have done, be it your partner, a friend, a colleague at work, or one of your kids, it will impact the relationship. Many people think that others don't know what they are thinking and feeling. Let me tell you, if you aren't saying it, you are likely showing it through your body language, what you *aren't* saying, and the things you avoid doing.

This state of anguish can rear its ugly head in situations where you internalize your feelings and struggle to communicate effectively to others what you need and want, or you lash out because of pent-up frustrations that haven't been resolved.

These feelings may stem from bitterness and unsettled issues that keep surfacing, dredging up negative emotions. Resentment can lead to mistrust in relationships and impacts your ability to *really* forgive, so you stay locked inside your very own prison.

When my kids were younger, before I sought a transformation of myself, there were many days I was NOT the person I wanted to be. As I have had time to reflect on myself, I can acknowledge it was because of all the pent-up frustration and anger I felt. I wasn't putting myself first, asking for help, or holding other people accountable for what they needed to do. And that is on me.

It is important to reflect on what might be causing those feelings and work through them so you can free yourself—and others—and find peace. Identifying what you are feeling resentment or anger about is important, although it can be painful to revisit. Consider toward whom you may be feeling resentment and what is causing it, which can help you begin the process of acceptance.

While this may not apply in all cases, in some, it may help to ask yourself what assumptions you are making about the situation or other person. Is there something you could learn that might help you understand the circumstances better? This is not about justifying the behavior of others, but it can help to gain additional context. Who do you need to forgive?

Redirect your energy. At times, there may be opportunities to leverage the feelings and energy you have toward something more productive. Consider coloring, painting or writing, which provide outlets to direct your feelings, ideas, and energy into creating something. While this may not be for everyone, it is an option to consider—on any scale—that will help you process your feelings and may even help other people heal from experiencing the very same thing.

Forgive yourself. When you peel back all of the resentment and frustration you have felt—which, let's face it, is usually aimed at other people, sometimes you are left staring at yourself in the mirror. And you may not like the reflection you see, not because of any physical imperfections, but because deep down you haven't released the anger you have toward yourself.

There may also be times when you are angry with yourself for how you handled a situation, or how you interact with some people, or you may be angry about how you got to a place where you put yourself last all the time. The first place to start is to acknowledge how you feel about yourself.

Consider where your behavior and actions toward others—and yourself—are out of alignment with who you want to be. Acknowledge the fact that everyone makes mistakes and the only way you can move forward is by identifying new behaviors to replace the old behaviors that weren't serving you so well. Practicing self-compassion is essential to work through forgiveness. Be kind to yourself; when you become aware that you are beating yourself up in your mind, tell that voice it isn't welcome anymore. Look in the mirror and tell that person you love her just as she is and for who she is becoming.

After all, resentment only ends up hurting the person with whom it resides.

Managing Barrier #4: The Need for Control

Acknowledge your need for control and understand its impact. One of the first steps to creating any change is awareness. Reflect on things that you are trying to control that are out of your direct span of influence or aren't priorities. That might include taking on too much, trying to control what people think or say, and even what people do. Think about how the need to control too many things is impacting you and those you care about. Then, explore what is driving the behavior and the consequences of your actions. Is it creating unnecessary stress for you, are you damaging relationships with others, etc.? Understanding the impact your need for control is having on you and others can help you evaluate if it is something that is important, and if so, to clarify so others can understand.

Identify triggers. What situations increase the likelihood of trying to gain control? Is it with certain people, or is it specific circumstances that cause you to step in and take over? Explore what you think will happen if you don't have control over that situation or person. What is the fear you have associated with it? This is another step to developing awareness so that you can identify what you need to change and when you need to implement new behaviors.

Identify the "stories" you are telling yourself. When people feel the need to control everything around them, there may be an inner dialogue occurring that is perpetuating false beliefs. What do you believe will happen if you don't have control? Could it be you don't believe it will be done as well, or fast enough? Could it mean that people may not need you, after all? Understanding the stories that you are telling yourself will be important to gain awareness so you can start rewiring your brain to believe otherwise.

Learn to let go. Identify when your thoughts and feelings create the need to control, then experiment with actions to work through it. This will take time, so be patient with yourself. Practice breathing techniques, use humor, and try writing down situations that trigger the need to control. Identify alternative actions to lessen your grip. I suspect you will find over time that when you begin to let go of the need to control so much, you will find it's not so bad to loosen up on the reins! You might find a bit of peace in the process.

When working through this area with my clients, they overcome this by letting go of things that aren't aligned with their priorities and goals. I worked with a female software executive recently who was involved in too many things at work, and her one goal was to feel relief. She wanted to prioritize herself more and focus on areas where she added the most value.

As we explored this more and identified the things she wanted to let go, she also reflected on the beliefs she was holding on to that were telling her what would happen if she did let go. To achieve this, we explored situations in which she might resort to old behaviors, which for her, were taking on too much or being involved in decisions that her team could handle on their own.

Some of the behaviors and thinking patterns she needed to work through included letting go of the belief that "If I'm not involved, then it won't get done," or "It won't be good enough...", and so on. It is thoughts like these that we all have and that can prevent us from achieving our next level of potential.

At times, your need for control could hinder someone else from growing. If you truly want to help others and you desire to help people develop, you need to explore if your actions are helping them or hindering them.

Managing Barrier #5: Excessive Deference

Reflect on your decisions. Think about the steps you take when making decisions. Do you constantly ask others what they think? Do you worry about upsetting someone by making a decision on your own? Do you feel the need to get permission from others to make decisions? Identify situations where you want to make more independent decisions so you can begin exercising more agency.

Clarify who owns the decision. Many situations at home and work require input from multiple stakeholders or some influencing to make the best decision, but generally, one person is responsible for making the decision. As you think about the types of decisions on which you tend to defer to others, identify which ones you believe are yours, and only yours, to make.

Trust yourself. There are situations where you instinctively know that it is the right thing for you. Whether you call that voice inside your gut feeling or a higher power speaking to you, listen to it. It can also be helpful to anticipate the position your partner or other important people will have about your decisions. Consider potential upsides for how those decisions will benefit them but be sure to anticipate what might cause pushback. This may increase your ability to influence their position to support your desired outcomes.

Take risks and be more decisive. Allow yourself to be vulnerable. Start small with situations you would consider low-risk so you can ease into taking bigger risks. If you are used to asking others for advice when making decisions, try making them yourself a few times and evaluate how you feel afterward. Consider what helped contribute to the success you had and identify what you could do differently next time and try it again. It is through this kind of practice that you increase confidence and develop stronger capabilities.

It can help to establish a few options that you can live with when making a decision, which can instill more confidence in your decision. Another strategy is to set a deadline as to when you need to make a decision, which can help you pull the trigger, so to speak.

Managing Barrier #6– Time Constraints

Take inventory. First things first: you need to identify where you are spending your time. You can start by keeping track of what you do for a few days or a week. Yes, I know, it seems like a lot of work, but I promise, you will learn something in the process. It will help you gain awareness of your patterns of behavior. Completing this exercise provides good data, which can help inform what changes need to be made.

Prioritize how you spend your time. We are all given the same amount of time each day, and our individual priorities are likely similar in some ways, but vastly different in other ways, depending on the season of life we are in. Your capacity to get things done is limited. Certainly, some days you may feel more productive than others and various things will contribute to that. Like the type of tasks on your to-do list, your energy level, and how long you anticipate they will take. There are some key strategies that I find helpful to prioritize and manage my time better, which are summarized below.

1. **Define your priorities.** Determine what is important and confirm you are aligning your efforts according to your vision.
2. **Identify what it will take to execute your priorities.** Determine your personal capacity, how much time it will take, and the resources needed to act—then leverage resources accordingly.
3. **Organize your priorities.** What needs to come first? Consider where your energy and effort are most needed, or what will be the most difficult. Getting the hard things out of the way first can be a game-changer.
4. **Act on your priorities.** Even if you find yourself procrastinating or are afraid to get something started, take one small step forward. Do something—this facilitates forward momentum and achieving results.
5. **Reflect on accomplishments and celebrate.** Step back and recognize progress toward your goals; this can help motivate you to continue pushing forward.

There are other considerations as you begin managing your time:

Elevate yourself: You need to be on your priority list. If you find the list is generally about other people and things, then I would encourage you to revisit your priorities based on what you identified in earlier chapters and what is truly important to you in life…and *for you*.

Know your prime time: Consider when you are at your best—the most productive, creative, and engaged. Is it at 5:00 in the morning that you tend to get a lot of things done before anyone else is up? Are you a night owl and prefer holding off on certain things until the evening, or do you prefer midafternoon to hit the ground running? You likely have a sweet spot each day where you are in your zone. It can be helpful to focus that time on the things that require your critical thinking and creativity. You have to gain some awareness about how you operate at your best and leverage those opportunities whenever possible.

Keep priorities visible: It is helpful so you can anchor your actions to align accordingly. Whether that is writing down your goals for the day, week, or month on your calendar or in a planner, or writing them on a sticky note on the fridge. Consider investing in a whiteboard at home. They are very visible and easy to write something down quickly, brainstorm, and erase things. It can also be a fun family tool to write each other sweet little notes or to-dos!

Find your flow: Learn to let go of things that don't align with your values and priorities, which means you need to say "no" now and then…or, at least, "not now". At times, people create urgency around things where there is none, or that urgency is assumed based on a request someone else has made of you. When someone asks you to do something, be sure to confirm when it is needed so you don't jump on doing it when it isn't required for another couple of weeks. One last important tip is to plan. This helps with projects at work (defining deadlines, people who are responsible, etc.) and at home as well as with planning meals for the week ahead. When you have food preparation planned out for the week, you will be a lot less stressed each night. If meal prep tends to fall squarely on your shoulders, try getting other people involved in planning and preparing meals. It creates opportunities to connect and have fun with your family.

Despite the barriers you may experience, what is critical is to develop your self-awareness and identify situations that prevent you from moving toward the goals you established for yourself. This helps you home in on situations where you can practice new behaviors to achieve your vision. It is amid adversity that you have the biggest opportunity to practice who you want to become. What are you waiting for?

What barriers are holding you back? Now that you have identified some of the common barriers people experience, which one(s) resonated most with you? In the space provided below, list what is getting in the way of becoming who you want to be and achieving what you want. Remember, you need to name it to tame it.

How can you overcome the barriers you are experiencing? Reflect on the barriers described in the previous exercise and the recommended actions you can take to overcome them. Describe below some of the actions you can take to move toward your vision.

KEY TAKEAWAYS

Principle #4: Amid adversity, you can reclaim power through choice.

1. Recover the inner strength you have always had—the power of choice.

2. Be confident in your conviction—then act accordingly.

3. When you encounter barriers, identify what you need to stay empowered.

4. Anticipate what you need to move through the discomfort of change.

5. Practice doing things differently and give yourself grace when you slip up.

PRINCIPLE #5

Peace prevails when you release what you can't control.

CHAPTER 13

Letting Go

*"The energy it takes to hang onto the past
is holding you back from a new life."*
– Mary Manin Morrissey

I was too tired to be my authentic self—I felt numb. This once spontaneous, fun, and exciting person was reduced to an exhausted and deflated mom, sobbing on the floor of her bedroom following what seemed to be a recurring argument with her son.

I. Give. Up.

Those words I have said many times in my head, but as many of you have probably experienced at some point, you can't. Yes, I have a lot to take care of and manage on my own. I must forgive myself. I must accept my imperfections and let go of the misperceptions and unrealistic expectations of others. I must let go. I was holding on too tightly to my own plan and missing out on what God had placed right in front of me.

I have realized that we all have unique life assignments that support a bigger plan and include other people around us. The most important of my life assignments is to raise my children and build their confidence so they can become productive members of society and leave a positive impact on generations to come. To achieve that, I must develop the best possible relationship with them. *How* I accomplish *that* requires me to understand their unique traits, disposition, triggers, and insecurities, as well as their wants and desires—while managing my expectations of what I want for them. It is so much more than "raising" children or being their provider and caretaker—I must also be a good leader for my children.

We all have our approach to parenting, and while I want the best for my kids and have visions of what their future could be, I am learning that it is not about what I want them to do or whom I would like them to become. Instead, it is to hone *their* ability to decipher who they are, what they want, and how they achieve things in life—and respect those around them.

I see my job as guiding, teaching, loving, and supporting them so they can learn to figure things out independently. What is not my job is to do the hard work for them. It is the work they have to put in to learn life's lessons. Allowing them to experience challenges and adversity helps develop their critical thinking skills to support the decisions they will eventually need to make on their own. It builds self-agency and confidence so they can move forward feeling more empowered.

Providing opportunities for your children to experience challenges and work through times of adversity is no small undertaking...particularly as a mom. "Why?" you ask. It's because oftentimes women step in to fix things to make them all better—when in reality it can prevent them from building the one thing we are trying to teach them—confidence in their abilities.

How can our children gain confidence, build problem-solving skills, and become independent if we are constantly there to step in when things get tough? Additionally, could this behavior—feeling the need to be everyone's caretaker and problem-solver when things aren't going as planned—be contributing to the stresses women feel around the caretaking responsibilities they have?

At times, what stresses moms is their tendency to try to carry a full load consisting of their lives *and* their children's lives. For some, they may fret about trying to solve everything for their children, which creates a tremendous strain on them—as they are not in control of their children's choices 24/7, and their answers may not be what the child chooses to do. I know this first hand, as I definitely fell into the trap of trying to control things—and even people—that were not mine to control.

Granted, this may depend on the age(s) of your child(ren), but as they get older, trying to control and manage every aspect of what they do and how they do it only further solidifies their dependency on you. How will it help them live their best lives if they constantly rely on you for everything?

An example I experienced was when my daughter was getting ready to go away to college. I had to be mindful of not telling her what I thought she should do in her career, what she should study at school, and even where to go. Of course, we had to set parameters and provide guidance to ensure she had the tools and guardrails to make a good decision. Of course, we were part of that decision. But what I didn't want was for her to look back and realize the "decisions" she made weren't her own. I didn't want her living her life based on what I wanted, or what her dad thought was best for her. We wanted her to make that decision for herself.

She chose a college that was the best fit for her and a field of study she is passionate about, which will ultimately help others. I see that in her actions, the confidence she demonstrates in her decisions, and how she is assimilating into college life. Watching my daughter over the last few months, since she has gone off to college, has been rewarding for me. It has also shown the growth I have experienced as a parent in letting go of things. She must now make decisions for herself and learn from them. While there are some decisions her dad and I will help her make, in many ways, I am not in control.

Reinforcing her dependence on me doesn't help me to prioritize what I need. And that has given me an unexpected sense of freedom.

Like with fingerprints, no two children are alike. As we see them grow from toddlers, we learn more, and with this, we know there are always positive rewards as they develop, as well as difficulties that come with growing pains. Since we can't necessarily select our children (taking only the good and leaving the perceived "bad" for some other parent to deal with), we must learn to adapt our approach based on the needs of our kids. This can be challenging at times as it requires us to adapt to the unique needs of others, stretching ourselves out of our comfort zone, and realizing maybe the "one size fits all" approach doesn't work all that well.

The need for adapting became more and more evident as I learned more about who my kids are as individuals and what they needed to be confident and successful in their own right. My daughter and son are different in many ways, so how I support and guide them needs to be adapted to their individual and unique needs. Like a leader adapts their approach to each employee on their team, parents need to adapt to their kids.

As I shared previously, my son Parker is neurodivergent. This means his brain operates differently than others who are considered "neurotypical". He learns and processes information differently and can behave in ways that may seem socially unacceptable. This is most often portrayed through his response when things don't go his way. His reaction might seem unreasonable or like he is overreacting. It took a long time for me to realize that I can't control his response to things. What I can control is my response to him, which if done well, can help minimize any perceived "overreaction".

As you might imagine, this experience has helped me realize that I can't parent my two children the same, nor can I worry about what other people think may, or may not, be going on with my child(ren). While some of my kids' needs may be alike, they are more different than they are similar, requiring me to adapt accordingly. Primarily, what I need to do differently with Parker is demonstrate a lot of active listening, patience, and managing my own expectations. He doesn't think or do things the way that I would, so I have to acknowledge that and meet him where he is. This is easy on some days, hard on most.

What I am most grateful for is where I am today, and what my kids have taught me. They have forced me to take a hard look at myself. I have developed much more patience as a result. I realized that I needed to focus on developing a good relationship with both of my children and not try to force them to do things or control their actions.

My approach to parenting doesn't always work. With the various responsibilities on my plate, my frustrations run wide and deep some days, and my response to those stressors is easy for everyone to see…and hear. I may not always do things the way others think is best or appropriate from a judgmental perch, but I do the best I can based on what I know and can do, at that moment. I am also fortunate to have learned from doctors, therapists, friends, and family—through what I put into practice and the environment I create at home. I know it will be a lifetime work in progress.

In the day-to-day grind of being a mom, I sometimes lose sight of the fact that my children will also adapt to me and the environment I create rather than what I want them to do or tell them to do. For example, if I come home from a hard day at work and walk into the house frustrated and looking drained, it permeates the rest of the house. My kids pick up that energy, which in turn, potentially causes them to react negatively or withdraw from me altogether. If this becomes a habit for me, it may impact my ability to build a healthy relationship with them over time. It's like those situations at work when you have to tell your boss something important, but you can see that they aren't having a good day, so you avoid interacting with them. Over time, this erodes trust in the relationship, impacts communication, and prevents the relationship from growing.

So instead of walking through the door after a tough day, and letting my kids see that my day wasn't great, I spend a few minutes in the car to reflect on what I want them to feel when I walk through that door—feelings such as, "Mom loves me and is happy to see me!" I can better prepare myself and create that positive experience for them. I might take a few deep breaths and focus my energy on what I will say and do when I walk in, or I might put on one of my favorite songs to shift my mindset to something more positive. Then, when I walk through that door, I can show up the way that I want to for my kids.

On a good day, I walk through the door and my son jumps into my arms, and he wraps his legs around me as he hugs me, showing how much he missed me too. I might kiss my daughter on her head (even if I get the "OMG, please don't touch me" look on her face!). At least I tried, and we might even get a good laugh from it. Much better than walking through the door in a bad mood, ruining the evening for myself and everyone else, including our dog. When there is tension in the house or someone is yelling, Nova often runs into the other room. That is how impactful our presence can be on others—and that is not who I want to be. How about you?

"Patience is the road to wisdom."—Kao Kalia Yang

Just as leaders in the workplace step in to carry out a task that isn't being done fast enough or well enough in their eyes, moms can do the same. I certainly have stepped in way too many times to fix something or make it just right—according to my standards. Or I have overreacted emotionally to situations with my kids, leaving me feeling like a "bad" mom. In doing this, I have also realized that I am robbing my children of the very thing that I believe I have been assigned to do. My life assignment is to prepare them for the real world. To do this, I have to encourage their independence so they can become masters of their destinies and learn about who they are and what they can achieve. In essence, I must let go of trying to control outcomes for them so they can be in the driver's seat. "How do you do this?" you ask. Through self-awareness and self-restraint, sprinkled with a lot of patience and asking thought-provoking questions so they can problem-solve on their own.

I recently had a visit from a friend who has a child around the same age as my son. As we sat talking, the kids went into the other room to play Xbox. As most kids experience when playing with others, it wasn't too long before they started to argue about whose turn it was to have the remote control. As their voices raised and the argument escalated, the discomfort the other parent and I were feeling was increasing with each passing second.

I started worrying about how my son was handling the conflict, and I could tell my friend was eager to jump out of her seat and see what was going on! The pressure to step in and help them work through it was palpable. For me, I was worrying about whether my son was giving a fair turn to his friend (knowing my son's tendencies). Though my friend said nothing, her facial expression said it all: she was worried about the same thing!

I have been in this situation repeatedly throughout my years as a parent and, in many cases, have stepped in, whether it was because I was worried about what the other parent would think of my kid (based on what they were doing at that moment), or what they were thinking about my parenting abilities based on how my kid was responding. After all, our kids are a reflection of us as parents, aren't they? I would argue against this point purely because we can't control what others do and how they respond. You may need to let go of what others think. Just stay the course you have set and trust in yourself.

When these moments occur on any given day and we do step in, it keeps us from prioritizing ourselves—especially when we do it repeatedly. I have concluded that one of the most important skills I have developed as a mom is the ability to manage my reaction and stay focused on being present in the moment. No, I have not mastered this, but I have realized that the issues others are having do not always require my attention, and when I can practice mindfulness amid chaos, it helps my sanity.

Wouldn't you know—despite the anxiety my friend and I experienced as our sons were disagreeing, they worked it out on their own. Sometimes, we let our own discomfort get in the way of our own growth, or worse, someone else's growth.

I share all of this with you because it is important to gain self-awareness around your own tendencies and how you operate—particularly under stress. In what situations do you tend to step in and take over? This is not an attempt to suggest that how you raise your kids or what you may be doing is wrong. Rather, it is intended to encourage you to reflect on where you are now, so you can evaluate if that is where you want to be.

What I realized about myself is I have always had a constant need to maintain a sense of control over everything around me. It was draining me physically, mentally, and emotionally. Worse, it was preventing others from achieving their own potential. This means I have had to let go of being involved in "everything" or having an opinion on "everything". While this will be something I will have to intentionally practice for the rest of my life given my personality and drive, I am moving in the direction of the personal vision I have for myself. One day at a time.

Living Abundantly

I believe it is part of true growth when we can learn to stop making everything so urgent and learn to let go, especially when most of that 'everything' is not all that important to begin with. The only true urgency is making each moment count toward your legacy and how you want to live your life. You never know how many heartbeats or ticks of the clock are left.

When your time is up, will you be able to say you have prioritized yourself and lived abundantly?

At this point in my life, I can honestly answer "yes," but I came too close to experiencing it on a flight with my daughter in the spring of 2023. We travelled to South Carolina to look at a few colleges. The flight was about an hour and forty-five minutes, and we were about thirty minutes from landing. I was in the middle seat, my daughter was in the window seat, and next to me in the aisle seat was a man—a very handsome man, I will add. I remember this vividly because he must've been about six-foot-five, and I recall thinking to myself that if anything happened, at least he would be able to help us open the door—as we were sitting in the exit row. I would be lying if I said I wasn't curious about how old he might be, and if he were single. But I digress.

I was doing some work on my computer when we suddenly hit turbulence. Bad turbulence. I'm not just talking about a few rattles. This was "My life flashed before my eyes" turbulence.

The plane dipped swiftly. People lifted up out of their seats. Flight attendants scrambled to find their seats. Then, the plane tipped sideways, as if the pilot was turning and then quickly decided to turn in the other direction. My computer slid off my tray. My daughter and I tried to make sense of what was happening, while also trying to figure out what our plan might be should things get worse. During those fifteen minutes of terror, I placed my hand on her leg and said a prayer. "God, please keep us safe. Please." As I said this prayer under my breath, many people were shouting and screaming. It sounded as if they were on the worst rollercoaster ride of their lives.

I looked over to the other side of the plane and saw people's drinks had spilled into the aisles. I heard one lady shout, "We are going to crash!" which was followed by more screams as other people started to question their own fate. This lasted for several minutes, which felt like an eternity. It was kind of ironic that I was almost faced with the decision of having to put my oxygen mask on first, before helping my daughter with hers.

Finally, the plane stabilized and righted itself. The flight crew came through the cabin to see if anyone needed assistance. There was stone silence. I suspect every single passenger realized we'd just come close to death. And yet, even amid the waning chaos and fear, I felt calm. I was keenly aware that it could have very well been my last moment, and weirdly, I was okay with that.

I wondered how I might have responded years ago when I was young and didn't have such an awareness of myself or my surroundings, or peace in my soul, as I did on that airplane. Would I have screamed as if it were my last moment on earth or would I have responded as I did this day, with peace and one last prayer? Would I have joined in the reaction of others, despite what I truly knew deep within my soul? Either way, I realized that I am at peace, no matter what happens. I feel I have lived a life of abundance. Getting here has required me to prioritize my own needs—sometimes over the needs of others. That experience was a reminder of how quickly life can be taken. I am going to continue living like there is no tomorrow.

Many of you may not want to face the fact that we are only on this earth for a limited time. Yes, you are dying. We are all dying—one day, anyway. When you consider situations like the one I experienced on that plane, it can happen to any of us at any time. So, I ask you, "Are you at peace with how you spend your time?" Are there things you want to do, or wish you had the guts to do? Are you elevating yourself as a priority?

CHAPTER 14

False Beliefs

"The truth of who we are is innate goodness, and the whole journey is really about removing any obstacle or false belief that keeps us from knowing that."
– Alanis Morissette

Despite your best-laid plans, sometimes things do not work out how you hoped, prayed, and dreamed. You labor over plans to create a desired future that can feel so out of reach…even fleeting. And sometimes you must let go to move forward, despite the feelings you have about what is within your grip—or just beyond your reach.

"Why dream, create goals, and establish plans?" you ask. Because it is through that process that you can see that you are progressing toward your vision, and being carved into the person you are meant to be and want to be. However, it is important not to secure your value, success, and worthiness to final outcomes. Otherwise, you set yourself up for disappointment. You are probably thinking, "Wait a minute! Didn't you tell me earlier to establish a vision and goals for myself? How can I let go of the outcomes I want for myself?"

It is inevitable that when you stay emotionally connected to things working out *just* right—the way you envision it in your head and the specificity around the details—you run the risk of being disappointed. I'm sure you have experienced a few of those missed marks yourself, whether it was the dream job you accepted that didn't really turn out to be what you expected, realizing the dream partner wasn't quite who you thought, or the fact that having a second child wasn't quite as easy as other people said it would be. I certainly experienced this when my life didn't unfold as I had planned: getting married at twenty-seven, having three kids, and buying a house with a white picket fence. When you focus so much effort on achieving the vision in your mind, perfectly, you miss out on enjoying the experience of where you are today and the excitement and unpredictability of what is yet to come.

Dreaming about your future and striving for something better helps motivate and propel you forward. It invites the opportunity to think as big as you want, to get excited about possibilities, and to plan out what *could* be. In the process, you must remain flexible about how you will get there and stay open to adapting courses and accepting how things actually turn out. Sure, there are situations where you achieve desired results—and those are moments to celebrate. However, it is important to remain open to other possibilities, as taking unexpected turns along the way can support your growth in ways you didn't anticipate.

Your own tendencies (i.e., personality, communication style, motivators, etc.) can keep you from living the life you crave, and if you don't pick up on it, you will likely find yourself still running on that hamster wheel.

In a recent conversation with a colleague of mine, who happens to be a very close friend, she identified that her drive for achievement and getting things done was preventing her from prioritizing time to do the things that truly fulfilled her in life. She was getting in her own way of creating the life she craved.

My friend is amazing. She has a kind heart, is passionate about supporting and developing others, and focuses on ensuring people's voices are heard, particularly people who are underrepresented and marginalized in our society. She is accomplished, emulates positive energy, is a great leader, and is not afraid to communicate her position on things. She is one confident woman, which is something I have always admired and respected about her.

We discussed her values and what is important to her, and one of the characteristics she used to describe her values was "achievement". Given all her career and personal accomplishments, she has definitely lived out that value in life. As we started discovering the things she wanted for her future, like traveling, spending quality time with her daughter, and other activities that focused on her personal renewal, she said something that stopped us both in our tracks.

She said, "If I'm taking time to prioritize the things I want to do, then the ball is getting dropped somewhere. I can't stop thinking about all the other things I should be doing at work." I repeated back to her what she said and added, "What is preventing you from doing the things you want for yourself?" She paused for a moment. My dearest friend stared up at the ceiling as she thought of her response.

Despite the discomfort I sensed her feeling at that moment, I could tell she was grateful to have the time, space, encouragement, and permission to reflect on these things. "It's my mindset," she said as if she had had an epiphany. "I have to focus more on being present with what I am doing and not worry about everything else I have going on."

We continued to discuss strategies to support the achievement of her goals and actions she could take to "let go" of the thinking that was keeping her from prioritizing the things she wanted for herself. She had to let go of the *belief* that if she focused on herself, other things would suffer.

The premise of this entire book is to help you understand that operating on autopilot and prioritizing other people and things is not sustainable. It will likely not fulfill you for very long, or if it does, it may have an impact on your overall well-being. Prioritizing yourself is about a mindset shift and doing the little things consistently each day—when it matters most—to achieve your personal vision.

Go ahead, moms. Fill your plate first.

CHAPTER 15

Grounded in Truth

RELEASE: WORKBOOK

"Your soul is always going to whisper your truth back to you.
Your soul wants what's best for you. And if you try to silence its voice,
eventually the whisper will become a roar."
– Lacey Johnson

As outlined in the five principles discussed in this book, my friend took time to reflect on where she was in life and where she felt out of alignment with her priorities. We identified her values, one of which was achievement, and she took time to rediscover what she wanted in her future. The obstacle wasn't necessarily about her time management; it was her mindset that was keeping her from moving forward and spending time on the things that she truly valued—and would create the change she craved.

One of the assumptions she made was that if she did the things that brought her joy, other things would suffer and reflect poorly on her—the self-proclaimed "overachiever". The challenge for her is reframing her thinking and working on staying present when she is doing the things she wants to do. *And* to be open to the possibility that taking time to herself to do the things that are a priority for *her* will make her better and stronger, allowing her to contribute more strongly in other areas.

She dreams of advancing in her career but worries her daughter and partner won't be supportive or will need her. That belief has been holding her back from exploring opportunities. I encouraged her to talk with her family, and what she learned through having that conversation is that they were very supportive, which gave her confidence and will empower her to make those decisions going forward.

When you practice letting go consistently, it allows you to show up with others in a more effective way. This is where the hard work comes in.

How are you getting in your own way? What must you let go of to move toward your vision?

Despite your best efforts to plan ahead to achieve what you want; your path can change on a dime. How you respond to that change matters. You never know what the future holds, and any sense of control you think you have about your future is just an illusion. Sometimes you have to trust and have faith that things will work out just how they are meant to, which may not be exactly how you envisioned them, but your experiences are pruning you to be prepared for what else lies ahead.

As I think about my perception when I was younger of what my life trajectory would look like, it was a straight line moving up from left to right—kind of like a chart an accountant shares that shows increased growth year over year (see illustration below).

Figure 2: Chart showing consistent, linear growth as goals are achieved over time.

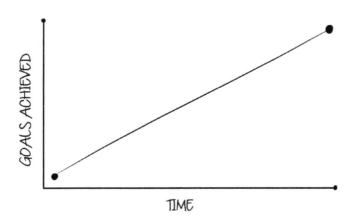

In reality, the graph that shows my true-life experiences is a bunch of ups and downs, zig-zagging with many highs and lows (see illustration below).

Figure 3: Chart showing inconsistent ups and downs as goals are achieved over time.

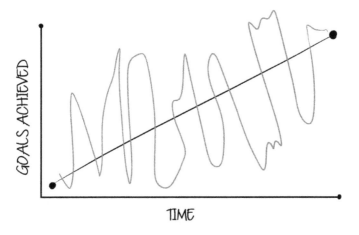

Yet when I reflect on the highs—like when I completed graduate school or got promoted at work, they didn't have as much impact as the lows. Yes, they were important and memorable, but they didn't necessarily help me grow into who I am today.

Rather, it is the low points on that graph—that suggest failure or "loss" instead of "profit"—that I remember the most. Like when I got divorced, or pregnant for the second time…unmarried. Or when I sold my house in CA, moved across the country by myself, and bought another house all on my own…and five months pregnant. I think you get the picture.

You see, my real growth took place during all of those low "zags" when I faced something unexpected—something that, at the time, I thought would break me. Worse, I didn't know if I had the strength to overcome the circumstances alone. But I did. And I can honestly say it is in those moments that I learned the most about who I am and what I am capable of. I would not be where I am today without those highs and lows, but what is essential to remember is that I had to learn from those low points. I had to develop more awareness of who I am, understand my pattern of choices that led me to those points, and choose to do things differently in some cases.

I could have let those challenges I experienced break me—and trust me, they nearly did—but if I reflect on my values, and step back to think about what I need to get through tough times, I can gain new perspectives and surround myself with what I need to persevere.

In the midst of adversity, we lower our expectations of ourselves and others. Or worse, give up altogether. It is in those moments that we need to lean into the discomfort of change and believe that we will make it out the other side—maybe even better, stronger, and closer to the vision of our future self.

As you move forward on your journey, I suspect you are wondering how you will be able to continue to move toward your goals but also manage your expectations along the way. Here are some additional questions to reflect on.

1. What barriers are in your way of achieving what you want?
2. What have you learned about yourself that is preventing you from moving forward?
3. What do you need to let go of, or be more accepting of?
4. What actions can you take to practice letting go or accepting?
5. Who/what can help you sustain the change?

If you could envision yourself sitting in a large auditorium, up on the balcony, and looking down on your past, what would you see? How would you view yourself and what could you say to that version of yourself, knowing what you know now?

What do you think she needs to hear? "I'm sorry for not listening to your gut when you wanted to...or felt the right thing to do was..." or "I'm sorry for not doing what you wanted—needed—but instead always put others ahead of you."

I don't mean to suggest it is about being sorry, per se; what I'm suggesting is that sometimes forgiving yourself frees you from ruminating on what was, could have been, or should have been—and move toward what you want.

I'm also not saying women should forget everyone and sacrifice the needs of others, particularly those who rely on you for life, health, and safety.

What I am saying is put your oxygen mask on first. If the plane is going down, you can't assist the person sitting next to you—particularly if it is someone who relies on you for their own well-being—if you pass out before you can help them.

Moms: eat first.

The following list describes success factors that may support you on your journey to creating the change you crave—and sustaining it.

1. **Stay in integrity.** Your biggest opportunity to work on becoming who you want to be is when you demonstrate old habits and behaviors that aren't serving you well. Think about situations you are most likely to give up or do the things you are trying to create change around—and be intentional in practicing new behaviors instead.

2. **Establish a support network.** Surround yourself with people who will support you and tell you the hard truths about what you might be doing to hold yourself back from your goals, lovingly and kindly.

3. **Get comfortable being uncomfortable.** Certainty brings security for many people, but when you don't know what the future holds or don't have control, it can create discomfort. Learn to do things outside of your comfort zone to build resiliency. Then, reflect on what helped you get to the other side and leverage it the next time.

4. **Acknowledge progress.** Take time to step back and look at how far you have come or identify the strength you are demonstrating amid difficult times. It is easy to lose sight when you are in the trenches fighting to make it through the day. Reflect on where you are going, and how far you have come, and consider adjustments you need to make.

5. **Have faith.** As with maintaining a growth mindset, faith is believing in something even when you can't see it—and keeping an optimistic perspective that new opportunities are always around the corner. Have a positive attitude and be open to what could be, recognizing that even if things don't turn out the way you hoped, you will still make it

through to the other side—and will be stronger because of it.

The inspiration for this book came primarily from my own experience but was supported by research, and further inspired by the stories of other moms who have similar lived experiences. What I do know is who I am, what I want more of in life, and what grounds me. These things are what make me unique and allow me to make decisions that are best for me and my family– rather than living up to the expectations others have of me. I hope you can find the same in your own personal journey.

As I write my last few pages of this book, I am enjoying my morning coffee in a mug that says, "This lady is one awesome mom", with an arrow pointing up (at me). It made me smile and realize that I *am* a good mom according to *my* definition and I deserve the opportunity to go after the things I want in life.

Reflecting on motherhood, yes, there have been many days where I was feeling "momgry". But I know that I did the best I could with what I had. I will continue until I take my last breath. I, too, will eat first.

Learning from the Past

Some days I reflect on how my mom must have felt raising my sister and me. I wonder if she had similar feelings to mine. I suspect she did, to some extent. I also realized that I had moments when I didn't always show my mom how much I appreciated her and what she did. In one instance, I did something cruel to my mom. Though it wasn't intentional, in hindsight, I think it was one of the worst things you could do to a parent—especially to a mom.

You see when I was in my first couple of years in college, I was given an award for Athlete of the Year. There was an awards banquet one evening, where I was going to receive the award. Most people would appreciate their parents being there to watch them receive the award, but not me. While I know both of my parents would have loved to be there and cheer me on, I didn't give my mom the opportunity. I didn't tell her about it at all.

When I played volleyball in high school, even throughout club and travel volleyball, and into college, my mom would embarrass me at my games. She would sit in the front row and when I was out on the court, she would scream my name, and you would hear her calling out plays, "Oh, Kathy! Get it, get it!" or she would stand and scream and clap her hands. It was so embarrassing.

When I got notified of the award being presented at the banquet, I immediately worried about her embarrassing me. A close family member, who was aware her behavior bothered me, suggested I not invite my mom because they knew how I would feel, so I didn't tell her about it.

My mom read about my award in the newspaper the next day. I have never felt so much shame in my life. I apologized to my mom profusely, but the damage had been done.

Fast forward many years later, when my mom was diagnosed with cancer and she was nearing the end of her life, I remember sitting on the bed with her. She lay in her bed with her knitted hat on to hide the fact that she had lost all of her hair. Her body was frail and very thin from treatment. Her zest and joy for life were slowly fading—but not in a way that said she didn't want to live anymore—she was more excited about going to see her savior, Jesus.

As I lay next to her, I can remember tears falling down my cheeks, reflecting on whether or not I had said what I needed to say, and if I had been a good kid for her. I told her how sorry I was for the things I had done to hurt her and recounted the volleyball award.

She spoke softly and whispered she loved me and not to worry. She knew I didn't get it at that age. I didn't understand at that point in my life that I would cause my mom tremendous pain by not including her—the one person who had essentially done everything for me growing up. I never felt her harbor any bad feelings about that, and in my mom's typical way, she told me that God would do good things in my life. That, I believe—but it took me a long time to forgive myself.

Despite the resentment we may feel when we don't think our kids understand all we do as moms, and that they are unappreciative, we have to step back and gain awareness. They don't always understand. It's generally not about their lack of care for us; it's about the fact that they haven't had the lived experiences you and I have had. That comes with living, learning, and gaining wisdom—if we are open to receiving it.

It has taken many years for me to gain the awareness I needed to grow more into who I wanted to become. That awareness allowed me to make better choices and prepared me for bigger and better opportunities. I have taken the time to step back, reflect, and evaluate if I'm heading in the direction I desire. It has not been easy holding the mirror up to myself, but I realize the more I do, the more comfortable I have become with who I am. I will continue to practice the five principles in this book and hope you have found them, and the exercises, useful on your journey.

Now, you know better, do better. Elevate yourself!

"In the end, only three things matter: how much
you loved, how gently you lived, and how gracefully
you let go of things not meant for you."
– Buddha

Next Steps: If you have done the exercises in this book, you have likely gained a lot of self-awareness. Now that you have more perspective, what do you need to let go of to move forward? Consider some of the false beliefs you may have identified earlier or other things that are misaligned with what you want.

KEY TAKEAWAYS

Principle #5: Peace prevails when you release what you can't control.

1. Identify what you can control and do it really well.

2. Have faith; let go of trying to control things, people, and outcomes.

3. Trust that you are where you are meant to be; it is a lesson.

4. Stay present and live in the moment.

5. Release the things that aren't aligned with where you are going.

Additional Resources

If you need help, there are a number of resources likely available in your community and through your job, many of which are confidential. This might include exploring benefits offered through your employer (Employee Assistance Programs, Employee Resource Groups, and counseling through your medical group). Below are some other resources to consider.

- You are not alone. Support groups provide a safe place for people in similar situations to find comfort. Ask a doctor or your state or local health department to recommend a caregiver's support group that offers virtual meetings. You can also find caregiver support resources by searching online and typing in "caregiver support group" and the name of your community. Childcare networks or eldercare support agencies for your state or county can also be contacted.
- Recognize when you may need more help. If stress or negative thoughts get in the way of your daily activities for several days in a row, talk to a psychologist, therapist, social worker, or professional counselor.
- Ask your doctor or local health clinic to refer you to counselors who may offer services for free or on a sliding fee scale. Some health insurance policies may cover counseling services.

- If you are feeling overwhelmed with sadness or anxiety, feel threatened, or want to harm yourself or others:

  o Call 9-1-1 for emergencies needing police, fire department, or ambulance.
  o National Suicide Prevention Lifeline dial 9-8-8, or call 1-800-273-8255
  o National Domestic Violence Hotline call 1-800-799-7233
  o National Child Abuse Hotline call 1-800-422-4453

If you are seeking support to help you on the journey of achieving your vision, Talent Principles offers a variety of development coaching and development programs for you to consider. You can find more information here: https://www.talentprinciples.com/.

Prioritize yourself.